WHY INNOVATION FAILS

WHY INNOVATION FAILS

FAILS

Hard-won lessons for business

Carl Franklin

First published in 2003 by
Spiro Press
17–19 Rochester Row
London
SW1P 1LA
Telephone: +44 (0)870 400 1000

© Spiro Press 2003

ISBN 1 904298 08 7

British Library Cataloguing-in-Publication Data.
A catalogue record for this book is available from the British Library.

Spiro Press USA
3 Front Street, Suite 331
PO Box 338
Rollinsford NH 03869
USA

Typeset by: Wyvern 21 Ltd, Bristol
Printed in Great Britain by: JW Arrowsmith Ltd
Cover image by: PA News
Cover design by: Cachet Creatives

Acknowledgements

This book has been the result of conversations with the following people, whom I would like to acknowledge and thank:

Jeremy Baker, Antonio Bernardo, Mike Bloxham, Robert Blyth, Paulina Borsook, Steven Brown, Simon Buckingham, Colin Burns, Nick Chater, James Chilcott, Phil Crawford, Ivan Diaz-Rainey, David Donnelly, Simon Duncan, Sue Eccles, Basil Englis, Christer Fåhraeus, Andy Gibbs, Dhruv Grewal, William Halal, Richard Harper, Stephen Harvey-Franklin, Dudley Hawes, John Hayek, JD Hill, Gerard Iannelli, Nick Jankel-Elliott, Tim Jones, John Keyworth, David Kirsch, Terri Kurtzberg, Olivia Landsberg, Gilad Lederer, Vivian Linacre, Alex Linden, Robert McMath, Paul Marks, Sarah Maxwell, Graham May, Don Norman, Richard Northedge, Terry Odean, Ian Pearson, Sue Robson, MJ Rose, John Ruggieri, Rudy Ruggles, Ilya Schiller, Carsten Schmidt, Randall Schultz, Narda Shirley, Ben Shneiderman, Jonathan Steel, Lucy Suchman, Steven Veldhoen, Tom Vierhile, Michael Watts, Tom Wells, Steve Whittaker, Helen Woodruffe-Burton.

I'd also like to acknowledge everyone else whose ideas I have discussed and whose words I have quoted.

Thanks are also due to all my friends for their encouragement and support; to my editor, Susannah Lear, for her endless patience and encouragement; and to my publisher, Carl Upsall, for picking up the phone.

Dedication

For my parents,
Avril and John Robinson

'The best laid schemes o' mice an' men,
Gang aft agley,
An' lea'e us nought but grief an' pain,
For promis'd joy!'

Robert Burns, November 1785

Foreword

This is one of the most extraordinary books on innovation I have ever read. It is crammed full of comments, quotes, quips and observations which will arouse and stimulate the innovator, helping them identify why innovation fails – and why it succeeds. As the inventor of the clockwork radio, this book makes particularly interesting reading for me because I have personally been through some of the experiences described – and realize that sometimes the only thing that carries you through is your own self-belief, tempered with a commercial reality. This book demonstrates the obstacles to successful innovation and, using real-life examples, shows how determined minds overcame them. Insights from history illustrate how taking ill-considered risks can also lead to calamity...

So, what is a great innovation? We are all great 'hindsight engineers'. However, often the people who say 'I could have told you that wouldn't work' have never created anything new in their lives. I have a favourite expression which I read somewhere in a book of quotations: 'I don't mind anyone looking down on me, as long as they don't expect me to be looking up.' Hindsight, of course, is all very well – and we can all criticize after the event. The lesson of this book, however, is to prepare thoroughly and listen to feedback *before* you act!

Innovation is a complex, demanding business, and it seems remarkable to me that anyone bothers to have a go. Society seems stacked against the innovator, determined to prevent the individual succeeding. However, one thing is clear to me – none of us as individuals has all the skills we need to bring a product or an idea to the marketplace. We need to collaborate, and we need to listen.

I hope there will always be room for the crazy inventor, but one tempered with market awareness and realism. After all, convention is an enemy to progress!

Trevor Baylis OBE

Contents

Introduction

Most books on the subject of innovation are written by academics, management consultants or product development specialists; as such, they tend to focus on 'the doing' of innovation and how to encourage a climate of innovation within large organizations.

The idea for this book came to me over a number of years. As a technology journalist who also covered the internet, it was my job to look at hundreds of innovative ideas for new products and new businesses during a boom that eventually went bust on an unprecedented scale.

Several things struck me during that time: there was a great deal of hype about promising new technologies that never really found a market beyond a handful of hardcore early adopters; lots of seemingly bright ideas came to grief and lots of obviously silly ideas got funding – and then flopped in the market.

These were not the products of stupid people – far from it. They may have failed in the market and failed to live up to the hype, but they must have made perfect sense at the time to the people behind them. So, for the purposes of this book, the definition of innovation is:

Innovation is anything that somebody thinks is a great idea.

Whether you're an inventor beavering away in your workshop or a product development bod beavering away in the office or laboratory, whether you're an investor or an entrepreneur planning to start a new business – be it a tea shop or a technology firm – this book is for you. What you're trying to do probably seems like a great idea, just as WebVan or Boo.com or the Sinclair C5 did to the people who dreamed them up. But the sad statistics of innovation are not on your side and the failure rate is depressingly high. Unfortunately, the reason so many seemingly great ideas flop is that when you look at them closely, they really aren't good ideas after all; and what is wrong is the thinking behind them.

So this book is all about the *thinking* behind innovation and the questions that innovators should be asking along the way. It won't tell you how to develop products, secure finance or file for patents. Nor will it tell you how to create a climate in which innovation can flourish. However, with any luck, it will equip you with a few more ideas and insights, and a few more questions that you ought to ask before you start.

The book kicks off with a look at how NASA managed to crash a spaceship into Mars because the US aerospace industry was clinging to an outmoded system of weights and measures that should have been replaced by the more modern metric system more than century ago. Yet the metric system has still to take off in the world's biggest economy, and for very a good reason – people simply don't think it's better, so why should they bother with it?

This 'so what?' factor has scuppered many a great idea, as we'll find out in Chapter 2 when we consider the long and distinguished history of failed innovations, from life-saving 'no-brainers' like sanitation and condoms to the electric car at the turn of the 20th century.

In Chapter 3 we'll ask what is meant by innovation and look at what has to go into something before it can be called innovative. Remember, innovation isn't just about new products; business strategies and social innovations like high-rise housing can seem like great ideas, but they too have a history of failure from which we can learn. After taking on board the lessons of failed innovations, in Chapter 4, we'll explore the reasons why innovations fail, from believing the hype that invariably surrounds new ideas (Chapter 5) to bad thinking on the part of innovators themselves (Chapter 6). Then in Chapter 7, we'll try to understand the apparently irrational reactions of consumers to innovations that really do seem like great ideas, and investigate why people hang on to the old ways of doing things and to old and outdated technologies.

In chapters 8–11, we'll cast a sceptic's eye over some of the much-hyped innovations of the recent past and near future, from robotic vacuum cleaners and internet fridges to online shopping and new computer interfaces. What we'll see is that many of them lose their lustre when we start to ask a few tough questions, but that's not to say they won't happen … eventually.

In the penultimate chapter, having explored why innovation fails – and with any luck having learned not to repeat the mistakes of the past – we'll end on an upbeat note and explore why innovation succeeds.

Finally, I'm going to challenge the notion that it's better to try and fail because that's what innovation is all about. I hope that reading this book can open your eyes to the fact that failure is avoidable, if only we apply a little critical thinking. I am not against innovation, just bad innovation.

It's a sad fact, but statistics are not on the side of the innovators and entrepreneurs. Billions are wasted every year on innovations that fail, because failure rates are depressingly high for new products, new services and new business ventures. But throughout this book are some tough little questions you should ask and some useful tools that you can use in order to reduce the risk and improve your chances of success. So, if you ask all the tough questions and it still looks like a great idea, then good luck and go for it! You deserve to succeed.

1

Why the metric system isn't rocket science

'Failure is not an option.'

Eugene Krantz
NASA Flight Director, Apollo 13

Innovation is a risky business; sometimes, great ideas just crash and burn. Not literally, of course, unless you happen to be referring to the Mars Climate Orbiter (MCO).

Mars Climate Orbiter was supposed to have been the first interplanetary weather satellite, designed to orbit the Red Planet taking measurements of its climate and relaying them back to earth. It was built by Lockheed Martin Astronautics of Denver, Colorado, as part of NASA's Mars Surveyor Programme, which included the Mars Global Surveyor and Mars Polar Lander satellites. All three spacecraft were designed under the agency's 'Better, Faster, Cheaper' philosophy, which was intended to boost the number of satellites exploring the solar system.

BETTER, FASTER, CHEAPER – CHOOSE TWO

Launched from Cape Canaveral on 11 December 1998, the Orbiter took 268 days to reach its target, where it was supposed to go into orbit through a tricky manoeuvre called 'aerobraking'. In effect, the satellite would dip into the upper reaches of the Martian atmosphere where its single solar panel would act as a brake, slowing it down over a period of days and helping it to achieve a more stable circular orbit. Unfortunately for NASA, things didn't quite go as planned.

Flight controllers at NASA's Jet Propulsion Laboratory (JPL) in Pasadena had originally planned for MCO to reach the planet at an altitude of around 226km, entering its aerobraking orbit before swooping around the far side of Mars. Just after 1am California time, on 23 September 1999, the Orbiter fired its main engine to begin slowing down. A few minutes later – as is the case when spacecraft fly around the far side of another planet – telemetry signals from MCO were expected to go dead until the satellite reappeared, some 21 minutes later. But the loss of signal happened 49 seconds early and the control team quickly realized that something was badly amiss. Tension rose as the minutes ticked by and the controllers waited nervously to see if the Orbiter's telemetry signals would kick back into life, confirming that the ship had made it safely round the planet. But when the time came, the radio waves were silent.

Fearing the worst, the JPL controllers fought to re-establish contact with the lifeless satellite, but to no avail. On 25 September, after two days of trying, they gave up. Mars Climate Orbiter had been lost.

WHAT WENT WRONG?

Immediately, an inquiry began into what had gone wrong[1]. Within days the navigators at JPL noticed there were discrepancies in the figures Lockheed Martin had been sending them to guide the spacecraft on its nine-month flight to Mars. They were in 'English' (ie 'imperial') units, not metric[2].

For Mars Climate Orbiter the consequences were catastrophic. By the time it reached its destination it was so much off course that instead of skimming into thin atmosphere more than 200km above the planet's surface, it flew into much thicker air just 57km above the ground. Travelling at 10,000mph, the Orbiter stood no chance of surviving; it literally burned and crashed. A $125 million spacecraft was turned into a meteor because nobody had realized that one set of rocket scientists was using imperial units, while the other was using metric.

What was surprising about this disaster was that NASA and its contractors were still using an unwieldy and confusing system of measurement dating back more than a thousand years. Why hadn't they adopted the more modern metric system, which was designed to make life easier for exactly the kind of people flying Mars Climate Orbiter?

The answers are contained in a report entitled *Assessment of NASA's Use of the Metric System*, which the agency's Inspector General published in February 2001. For anyone studying why innovation fails, it's a fascinating case study; but first we have to put the metric system's 'big idea' into its proper historical context.

THE METRIC SYSTEM

The metric system arose from efforts in 17th and 18th-century Europe to produce a standardized system of weights and measures that everyone could use and understand[3]. At the time, Europeans were using a hotchpotch of measuring systems drawn from a variety of earlier cultures – Babylonian, Roman, Egyptian, Anglo-Saxon and Norman. With such a diverse heritage came a confusing array of basic numbers with which to work. The Romans used base 12 – or duodecimal – numbers with the foot of 12 inches, and in Roman times, 5,000 feet made a mile. In fact, the foot was something of a flexible measure, depending on where in the world you stood. In the Celtic lands of Scotland and Wales there was a ploughman's foot equivalent to 9.5 modern inches, the Roman foot was 11.53 modern inches, in Greece it was 12.45 inches and in Poland it was 14[4]. The inch we now know and love was standardized in the reign of King Edward I (1272–1307) as the length of three barleycorns, which in turn gave a standard measure of a foot.

Three feet made a yard, which King Henry I of England had earlier defined as the distance between the tip of his nose and the end of his outstretched thumb. Twenty-two yards made a chain and ten chains made a furlong. For some reason, Queen Elizabeth I decided it would be convenient for eight furlongs to make a mile, so she decreed that henceforth, the Roman mile of 5,000 feet would be replaced by the 'statute' mile of 5,280 feet[5]. Of course, the statute mile should never be confused with the 'nautical' mile, which is 6,080 feet long.

Imperial measures

1 link	=	7.92 inches
1 foot	=	12 inches
1 yard	=	3 feet
1 rod or pole	=	25 links or 5½ yards
1 chain	=	4 poles
1 furlong	=	10 chains or 40 rods
1 mile	=	8 furlongs or 5,280 feet
1 nautical mile	=	6,080 feet
1 ounce	=	16 drams
1 pound	=	16 ounces
1 stone	=	14 pounds
1 hundredweight	=	8 stones (112lb)
1 ton	=	20 hundredweight (2,240lb)
1 short ton	=	2,000lb
1 gill	=	2 tots
1 pint	=	4 gills
1 gallon	=	8 pints

Source: *A Guide to Customary Weights and Measures,* British
Weights and Measures Association

If this wasn't mystifying enough, the basic unit of weight in Olde England was the grain – a barley grain, in fact – of which 7,000 made a pound unless, of course, it was a Troy pound, which consisted of 5,760 grains. Sixteen drams made an ounce, 16 ounces made a pound and 14 pounds made a stone. A hundredweight was really 112lb and a ton was 2,240lb unless, of course, it was an American 'short ton' of 2,000lb.

Liquids and volumes presented an equally bewildering array of measures, with one gallon (eight pints) originally being defined as the volume of eight pounds of wheat. A gallon of water in Britain occupies 277.274 cubic inches, while in the US it takes up 230. Confused? You should be!

Now, imagine you're an entrepreneur living in Europe, some time in the 17th or 18th century. You've seen all this confusion and you've tried adding in bases 12, 14 and 16 and decided it was all too complicated, so you come up with something simpler. What you propose is a new and innovative system of weights and measures standardized around base 10 arithmetic and water.

Here's how it works: one metre is 100 centimetres long and a volume of water that's $10 \times 10 \times 10$cm is 1,000 millilitres or one litre. Each millilitre weighs one gram, so 1,000 cubic centimetres weighs 1,000 grams or one kilogram. After that it's just a case of moving the decimal point around and putting another fancy prefix in front of metre, litre or gram. Add a few more decimal units for stuff like temperature and pressure and hey presto! You've got a system of weights and measures that'll do for measuring anything between a Buckyball and a galaxy. What's more, there are no inconvenient numbers like 12, 14, 16 or 22 and no weird fractions to deal with because everything is decimal and base 10 arithmetic is the easiest of all. What a great idea!

With such an innovative notion, the chances are that you'd draw up a business plan and rush it round to your local venture capitalist. You'd explain to him that the business model involves giving away the system of measurements to build up the user base, then licensing the measuring technology itself so that every ruler, pint glass and set of scales will generate a royalty. At this point, seeing the potential to create a worldwide standard of weights and measures, the venture capitalist would probably start babbling about 'the new economy' and dollar signs would pop up in his eyes – just like they do on cartoons! After all, who could resist a no-brain innovation like this?

METRIC MIRE

As we now know, the big idea didn't exactly take off like Netscape. Although the Dutch mathematician Simon Stevin first suggested standardizing weights and measures around base 10 numbers as early as 1585 (in his book

De Thiende), it was another 85 years until a French astronomer and priest, Gabriel Mouton, laid the foundations of the modern metric system. He took the decimal idea a stage further by suggesting a basic unit of length related to a tiny fraction of the Earth's circumference – one minute of arc, in fact, which is roughly equal to a nautical mile.

But Mouton's ideas went unheeded at the time and it was a further 125 years before the French Academy of Sciences created the metric system as we know it today[6]. The metre they defined was equal to one ten-millionth of a quadrant of the circumference of the Earth, measured between the North Pole and the Equator along a line running somewhere between Barcelona in Spain and Dunkirk in France. Obviously, this was a big improvement on measuring the outstretched arm of a king. The metre has since been redefined as the distance travelled by light in a vacuum over a period of 1/299,792,458th of a second.

Though France officially adopted the metric system in 1795, the Emperor Napoleon suspended its use in 1812 and it wasn't until 1840 that metrication was revived for everyone to enjoy. Well, not everyone, because despite the apparent advantages of the metric system – and more than 200 years after its invention – Britain and the US have yet to embrace it wholeheartedly.

Although the US has officially recognized metric units since 1875, when it signed the Treaty of the Meter, it remains the only major country still to adopt its modern form, the International System of Units (SI) as its official standard of measurement. Being 'the preferred system of weights and measures for United States trade and commerce' since 1988[7] has done little to help the spread of SI units across the world's greatest industrialized nation. As NASA's report points out: 'Use of the metric system is voluntary and Congress has created no deadline for conversion.'

WHY NASA ISN'T METRIC

Across the space agency itself, metrication has been patchy – even though it has been the 'preferred system' for all new projects since 1991! Although NASA's scientific community has almost entirely gone over to using SI units,

its aerospace engineers still prefer to use imperial. The International Space Station is a hybrid project using a mixture of SI and imperial but the Space Shuttle is purely imperial. NASA's most progressive adopter of SI is the Jet Propulsion Laboratory, where just 32% of projects use it exclusively.

In its report on metrication across the agency, NASA found that the barriers to its adoption of SI units were both real and perceived. Firstly there was the cost of switching, because all the precision instrumentation and software would have to be changed from imperial to SI. (Although not insignificant, I bet it would have cost less than the $125 million that went up in smoke when the Mars Climate Orbiter crashed!)

Then there was cultural and psychological resistance: engineers who had grown up with the imperial system felt uncomfortable using metric units and believed a lot of their 'intuitive knowledge' would be lost. This, in turn, would add a degree of risk to mission operations as engineers struggled to make sense of an unfamiliar system of measurement. It was for this reason that older engineers at NASA frequently encouraged younger colleagues to work in imperial, even though they may have been trained in the metric way of thinking. So much for reducing risks!

A more serious obstacle to metrication is the fact that America's aerospace industry is firmly in the imperial camp, with little intention of moving. Lockheed Martin, for example, was working in 'pounds of force', but the Jet Propulsion Laboratory was expecting navigational data in Newtons. With one pound of force equalling 4.45 Newtons, the navigators' subsequent calculations were out by a factor of 4.45, which is why the spaceship crashed.

Because the aerospace industry doesn't work with metric units, it has little need for metric parts, as the NASA report observes:

'Even when engineers use the metric system in the design process, the lack of aerospace-quality standard parts and components (such as fasteners and valves) makes implementation of fully metric designs difficult. The lack of metric hardware results from the realities of the market economy – until a demand exists for qualified metric parts, technical standards and reference data, these items will not be generated. A metric NASA project, by itself, is typically too small to influence the manufacturing community to increase the availability of metric parts.'[8]

So, NASA's failure to adopt the metric system and use it in the kind of high-precision scientific environment for which it was ideal came down to a combination of factors: switching costs, perceived risks, corporate vested interests, industry standards, user psychology and a shortage of widgets!

Interestingly, of the eight recommendations made in the Inspector General's report, not one addressed the psychological barriers to adoption that existed among NASA's engineers. What's more, the agency decided not to mandate the use of SI in its interactions with the public, especially when it was referring to projects that used exclusively imperial. That doesn't exactly make it a good role model and, as we'll find out later, good role models – or change agents – are crucial to the success of any innovation.

AMERICA'S METRIC EXPERIENCE

NASA's experience with the metric system is typical, in a country that has yet to mandate its use. The US flirted with the idea early in the 19th century when no less a man than John Quincy Adams delivered his *Report on Weights and Measures* to Congress in 1821, four years before he became President.

Describing imperial measures as 'the ruins of a system, the decays of which have been repaired with materials adapted neither to the proportion nor the principles of the original construction', Adams called for a sustained international effort to standardize weights and measures around the world.

But he also admitted:

'It is doubtful whether the advantage to be obtained by any attempt to apply decimal arithmetic to weights and measures would ever compensate for the increase in diversity which is the unavoidable consequence of change.'[9]

If converting an entire country over to the metric system seemed daunting back in 1821, just think how much more difficult it would be today.

But the man once charged with encouraging the US to switch is adamant that the metrication programme is succeeding. 'I don't think the metric effort has failed here,' says Gerard Iannelli, former Director of the Metric Program at the National Institute of Standards and Technology. 'One reason we haven't gone all the way is that it continues to be a voluntary transition.'

In fact, Iannelli points out that three transitions are under way, albeit with varying degrees of success. Trade and commerce is the main focus of government efforts, so that American companies can benefit from using the same language of measurement as the rest of the world. Many pockets of resistance still remain, however, the aerospace industry being the most notable.

Education is the second battleground, according to Iannelli. 'It's going smoothly in schools,' he says of the efforts to teach the metric system to the next generation of Americans, 'but if it's not reinforced by their parents we're losing out in the third area of transition, which is our culture.'

And there's the rub: in the routine of our daily lives, those of us in supposedly 'non-metric' countries encounter the metric system a lot more often than we might imagine. The food we eat comes in pre-packed ready meals without a hint of pounds and ounces on the packaging. We wash it down with Coke poured from a two-litre bottle and pig out on Cherry Garcia from a 500ml tub.

But our road signs are in miles, we order beer by the pint, eat 16oz steaks and weigh our apples in pounds, and none of these everyday encounters with weights and measures has anything to do with scientific precision or international trade. They are, however, potent symbols of the old imperial order – far more visible to us than the 400g lasagne we bung in the microwave without so much as a second glance. Metricate our ready meals and nobody gives a damn; metricate our fruit, however, and it looks like a revolution.

METRICATION CATCHES ON IN THE COMMONWEALTH ...
BUT NOT IN BRITAIN

Some revolutions pass without any great upheaval. Canada's relatively painless transition to metric road signs back in 1977 was documented in the *Transportation Research Report*, which attributed the campaign's success to eight years of planning and a high-profile public education programme with strong support from the government[10]. Road signs were changed almost overnight and an overwhelmingly supportive public had few problems making the mental adjustments. Since then, however, Canada's wider metrication campaign has lost momentum and the country – which cherishes its French heritage so much – has still to convert fully.

Another outpost of the Empire had a surprisingly trouble-free transition to metric in the early 1970s. In July 1974 almost every road sign in Australia was converted from miles to kilometres following an intensive public awareness campaign. By the end of the year, the teaching of SI units was compulsory in schools and almost every family in Australia had been bombarded with pamphlets explaining how the conversion affected them. Several years later, however, a report by the Australian Metric Conversion Board noted pockets of lingering resentment, because people were reluctant to forget a system of measurement they had been using all their lives.

On this, the *Transportation Research Report* observes:

> 'The Board failed to grasp that metrication involved a substantial cultural change. Common sayings (miles per gallon, an ounce of prevention, etc) could not be readily replaced in metric terms.'

As to the British experience, this short extract from the *TRR* document just about sums it up:

> 'The metric conversion process in Great Britain began in 1965 and evolved slowly for more than 10 years before grinding to a halt.'

In fact, metrication was actually *banned* in 1975 as far as public projects were concerned and government apathy ever since has ensured the right of

Englishmen to drink *pints* of warm beer while enjoying a game of cricket played out on a wicket of 22 *yards*. The national psyche was captured in the conservative *Daily Telegraph* newspaper, which commented in July 1995 that metrication was 'not just a practical conversion: it is political, virtually a spiritual, conversion.'

METRICATION BY STEALTH

The reality is, of course, that Britain and its ready meals have since gone metric by stealth, and thanks to legislation imposed by Europe, British grocers now face prosecution for measuring fresh produce on imperial-only scales. Those defying the law have ended up in court, feted by papers like the *Daily Telegraph* as 'metric martyrs'!

Pondering on why the non-adopters resisted metrication, the authors of the *Transportation Research Report* make this intriguing observation:

'Whether it was apathy, an incomplete public relations program, or some other factor, many people continued to use imperial measurements and to resist using the metric system. They did not grasp the advantages of the metric system and did not understand that it was a better system.'

But with metrication facing so much resistance in some of the world's strongest economies, it begs the question whether the metric system actually *is* a better system; in short, is it really an innovation?

WHAT DEFINES AN INNOVATION?

The classic definition of what characterizes an innovation comes from a book entitled *Diffusion of Innovations* by Everett Rogers, a professor of communications and journalism at the University of New Mexico.

He argues that anything claiming to be innovative should be judged against five important criteria that will influence its spread throughout society[11]:

● **Relative advantage:** Do people think it is an improvement over what already exists?

- **Compatibility:** Is it consistent with the values, experiences and needs of the people who might adopt it?
- **Complexity:** Will potential users find it easy to use and understand?
- **Trialability:** Can people experiment with the innovation before deciding to adopt it?
- **Observability:** How easy is it for people to see its results?

It's immediately obvious from Rogers' definition that the characteristics should be judged *by the user*, not by the innovator. Compare this with the *TRR* comment about non-adopters of metrication and you'll see an example of what Rogers calls a 'pro-innovation bias' in the language; those who resisted 'did not understand that it was a better system' (the implication being that they were at fault, not the metric system itself!).

A better system – for whom? Obviously not the people who resisted metrication because otherwise they would have adopted it with enthusiasm, just as they had adopted washing machines and ready meals.

The metric system is certainly trialable and its results very observable. The measuring devices we use in our everyday lives – things like rulers, speedometers and scales – are usually in dual units and we can easily see how many centimetres are equal to a foot or how many pounds equal a kilogram. But to learn a new system on top of the familiar measures we already know adds a layer of complexity that many people consider unnecessary. Why forego and forget a perfectly good arrangement that has served us since we were young? Why invest the time and effort to learn something that, for most people, has little relative advantage? We are not scientists carrying out precision experiments.

A MEASURE OF ORDINARY LIFE

The fact is that, for most of us, a decimal system of weights and measures offers few advantages over the more cumbersome notation of imperial, and the reason for that is that we rarely have to think about the figures in our everyday lives. We buy ready meals in packs and soft drinks in bottles, and what matters is not the precision of their weight, but the fact that they look about right for our needs. When we buy a 12oz steak and a pound of sausages, we don't add the figures together to tell us we're carrying a pound and three-quarters of meat, because most of the time we really don't need to know. When we go to the filling station the fuel may be dispensed in litres, but most of us simply fill up the tank or put in a certain amount of money – we don't measure out 10, 20 or 35 litres. Out on the road, kilometres have no advantages over miles because both are base 10 numbers and the highways of Britain and the US are not full of tourists from Europe.

USEFUL NUMBERS BY HALF

While there is an undoubted elegance to the mathematics of decimal numbers, it's worth considering why numbers like 12 and 16 have done us so well in the past. Five hundred years ago our requirements for numbers were much simpler than they are today. Our ancestors weren't carrying out precision engineering, they were trading in day-to-day items using basic fractions like halves and quarters, because that was a convenient way of dividing things up. Look at the number 10 and see how many times you can halve it and still have a whole number. Now look at the number 12: it divides into 2, 3, 4 and 6 without any need for a knife. Sixteen is even better because it repeatedly halves into 8, 4, 2 and then 1.

In his *Report on Weights and Measures*, John Quincy Adams comments on this deficiency of base 10 numbers:

> 'Decimal arithmetic is a contrivance of man for computing numbers and not a property of time, space or matter. Nature has no partialities for the number 10 and the attempt to shackle her freedom with it will forever prove abortive.'

So for most people in the laggard nations of Britain and the United States, the decimal elegance of the metric system offers little advantage over its clumsy but culturally ingrained and apparently satisfactory rival. As the NASA experience has shown, if rocket scientists don't use the metric system to fly the Space Shuttle, then why should the rest of us bother?

What the loss of Mars Climate Orbiter highlights is that innovation is in the eye of the beholder. What's more, our perception is clouded by our cultural heritage, by our education, our political goals, our corporate vested interests and by the silly, irrational foibles of everyday life.

The metric system may be a great idea, but so what?

IDEAS FOR INNOVATORS

- Just because it's a great idea doesn't mean it will succeed. You may think your innovation will improve someone's life, but the fact is, your opinion doesn't count: theirs does!
- Smart people sometimes make stupid mistakes. The people flying the Mars Climate Orbiter really *were* rocket scientists.
- Is the metric system a success because most of the world uses it, or a failure, because America doesn't?
- Emotion, habit, culture and standards are difficult things to change. The metric lobby has been trying for more than 200 years.
- What's good for business may not be good for consumers.
- If you'd just invented the metric system, how would you pitch it to a venture capitalist? Would you bother?
- What do you think market research would say about metrication? Whom should we ask? Should governments press ahead with metrication even if research shows no desire for it?

NOTES

1 The record and analysis of what happened to MCO is contained in the NASA document *Mars Climate Orbiter, Mishap Investigation Board, Phase I Report*, published on 10 November 1999.

2 The NASA report refers to them as 'English' units, but the English invented the system and call them 'imperial'.

3 The metric system is properly known as Le Systeme International des Unites (SI) or the International System of Units.

4 A good description of ancient systems can be found in *A Guide to*

Customary Weights and Measures, written by Vivian Linacre, of the British Weights and Measures Association.

5 Source: *A Brief History of Measurement Systems,* National Institute of Standards and Technology.

6 The International System of Units (SI) was actually introduced in 1960 with six fundamental units: the metre, kilogram, second, ampere, kelvin, candela. The mole was added in 1971. Note that Celsius and litres are not regarded as fundamental units in SI, although they are an important and visible part of the wider metric system.

7 Public Law 100–418, the Omnibus Trade and Competitiveness Act of 1988.

8 Page 6

9 From the *Report on Weights and Measures,* 1821, quoted in Linacre.

10 Daniel S Turner, Jay K Lindly and Rodney N Chester, *Citizen Concerns and Public Awareness: Metrication examples. Transportation Research Report 1552.*

11 Everett M Rogers, *Diffusion of Innovations.* The Free Press, New York, 1995.

2

A brief history of *so what?*

'Most innovations, no matter how inspired,
end up on the scrap heap of history.'[1]

Michael Schrage
Co-author of *Serious Play* and research associate at MIT

The United States may be a laggard when it comes to decimalizing its weights and measures but it was an innovator when it came to decimalizing its money. Although the early settlers used English, Spanish and French currency, the War of Independence and the new Constitution spurred America into creating a currency of its own. Congress passed the Mint Act in 1792 and America became the first country to adopt a decimal system of currency, with one dollar made up of 100 cents.

It was a further 179 years, however, before Britain went decimal. Before 1971, the British system of currency, commonly known as '£SD', was based around a pound of twenty shillings and a shilling of twelve pennies, so one old pound was made up of 240 pennies, not 100 as in the decimal system.

Parliament had considered decimalization before – in 1824, 1853, 1857 and 1918 – but rejected the idea every time. The forecaster Paul Saffo, a director of the Institute for the Future in California, could almost have been talking about Britain's indifference when he told *InfoWorld* magazine:

'Never mistake a clear view for a short distance. Just because something seems terribly obvious and terribly necessary, it doesn't mean it's going to happen quickly.'

So, eschewing the computational elegance of base 10 book-keeping in favour of the established but cumbersome duodecimal arithmetic of £SD, the 'nation of shopkeepers' carried on grappling with figures like 'two and ninepence' until the decimal system finally arrived. From then on it was fourteen pence.[2]

Even so, there were gripes, as John Keyworth, Curator of the Bank of England, recalls: 'Decimalization seemed to represent such an enormous change that it spawned irrational fears about its implications,' he says of the national outcry in the run-up to D-Day. In fact, they proved entirely unfounded and the changeover went very smoothly.

Thirty years later and conservative Britain is once again a laggard, declining to join the single European currency – the euro (€). Like the metric system, the euro is an innovation that suffers from being 'not invented here'. The pound, by contrast, has been around for a very long time. Even though it was decimalized, it is still the pound, and it's *British*. John Keyworth explains: 'The pound was an Anglo-Saxon concept that was deeply ingrained in the culture of the country and had been so for around 1,300 years. It remained inviolate for more than a millennium, never having to be replaced by a new pound or any other designation, unlike the French and German currencies.'

Whatever the advantages of the single European currency – the British will no longer have to change pounds into pesetas when they fly off to Ibiza or trade with companies in Madrid – the euro is likely to encounter more resistance than decimalization ever did! At least the UK government has promised to hold a referendum – the ultimate form of market research – to see if anybody wants it!

WALL STREET'S FRACTIONS

Just in case any Americans are chuckling about dinosaur Brits holding on to an outmoded system of counting money, they might stop to think about the last bastion of free trade and elegant numbers – Wall Street.

Despite the fact that dollars have 100 cents, enabling shares to be quoted in convenient numbers such as $1.10 or $1.65, the stock markets clung on to fractions until April 2001. Not content with simple halves and quarters, Wall Street's finest were happy to work with 32nds and even 64ths, and many were doing the sums in their heads! So much for the convenience and innovation of decimal fractions – the brokers didn't want it.

One possible reason they resisted for so long was the 'spread' – the difference between the price at which the broker buys and sells. With the old system, share prices jumped discretely between fractions. Typical shares were quoted with a 'minimum price variant' of a sixteenth of a dollar, so there were 16 price points per dollar. A broker might buy for $10¼ and sell for $10⁵⁄₁₆, and the difference is 6.25 cents. After decimalization, the minimum price variant was reduced to a cent and so there are now 100 possible price points for a share. The impact of this was that the spread could be reduced to as little as a cent, so the broker's mark-up was reduced, along with his profits.

Both metrication and decimalization were innovations that came up against deep-rooted cultural resistance and the antipathy they faced was compounded by the considerable cost of switching. There may be a long-term economic benefit to standardizing weights and measures or switching to decimal currency, but converting road signs to metric is unlikely to pass even the most simple cost-benefit analysis.

EVEN LIFE-SAVING INNOVATIONS CAN FAIL

Even when the benefits of an innovation are both obvious and compelling – it saves lives – it's astonishing how humanity can still find seemingly irrational reasons to resist!

Take condoms, for example. Condoms have been around since the 14th century, when it was known that animal membranes acted as a barrier to sexually transmitted diseases. It was only later, in the 16th century, that people began to use them as a method of birth control.[3] Nowadays, modern latex condoms are one of the primary weapons in the fight against HIV/AIDS – a disease that has claimed the lives of more than 20 million people. More than five million people became infected in the year 2000 alone, bringing the total number of cases to around 40 million.

It wouldn't be exaggerating to say that sexually transmitted HIV/AIDS could be stopped in its tracks if men would only take the precaution of using a condom – a simple, cheap and reliable means of prevention whose effectiveness has been proved *beyond doubt*.

Tragically, however, the use of this centuries-old innovation is still being resisted: why? The most frequently-cited reasons can be found in a briefing document produced by Family Health International and supported by UNAIDS:

> 'Lack of sensation or interrupted sexual pleasure; psychological and social factors, including couple communication and assumptions that condoms are for use in extra-marital relationships and with prostitutes; lack of availability of condoms, including policies that prohibit condom distribution to youth; and a lack of confidence in the reliability of condoms themselves.'[4]

So, being simple, cheap, effective, reliable and *life saving* is obviously not enough to make people use them. Condoms are an innovation that saves lives, but so what?

IGNORING THE CURE FOR SCURVY

Another life-saving innovation that struggled against indifference was the use of lemon juice as a cure for scurvy. Despite being cheap, simple, effective and proven, this innovation was ignored for nearly 200 years – a delay that cost the lives of thousands of sailors and jeopardized the defence of the realm.

Throughout history, scurvy had been a major killer, particularly on longer voyages. What should have been a breakthrough against the disease came in 1601, during the voyage of four ships from England to India, under the command of Captain James Lancaster. On three of the ships, scurvy claimed the lives of 110 out of 278 sailors before they had even reached halfway. On the fourth ship, however, all the crew remained healthy because Lancaster was conducting a 'clinical trial' of lemon juice – three teaspoons a day for each man.

Despite Lancaster's success – the results he obtained were not just observable, they were blindingly obvious – the navy ignored his innovative cure. Thousands of lives later, in 1753, a surgeon named James Lind published *A Treatise of the Scurvy*, which seemed to settle the matter once and for all. In it, Lind described how in 1747 he performed a controlled experiment on 12 sailors aboard a ship called the *Salisbury*. All exhibited the symptoms of scurvy, which Lind observed as 'putrid gums, spots and lassitude, with weakness of their knees.'

With six different remedies to try out, Lind split the men into pairs, giving them a common diet of gruel, mutton broth, biscuits and dried fruit. To each pair he gave a different remedy:

- a quart of cider a day
- elixir vitriol
- vinegar
- sea water
- two oranges and a lemon
- nutmeg mixed with garlic, mustard seed and balsam of Peru.

Almost immediately, the sailors given the citrus fruit began to improve. Lind remarked:

'The most sudden and visible good effects were perceived from the use of oranges and lemons; one of those who had taken them being at the end of six days fit for duty.'

He later concluded:

'The result of all my experiments was that oranges and lemons were the most effectual remedies for this distemper at sea.'[5]

Despite the publication of the *Treatise* and its eminently repeatable experiments, the navy continued to ignore the cure for scurvy until 1795 – 42 years after the *Treatise* and a full 194 years after Lancaster's first experiments. It's worth remembering that these were the days when naval power was crucial for the execution of war and the defence of the realm. But the widespread loss of life and the threat to national security seem to have been insufficient imperatives for the navy to adopt a workable cure for one of its most devastating problems. Just imagine how history might have turned out if all British sailors had been kept in good health by the simple innovation of lemon juice!

What finally stirred the Admiralty into action was the influence of Gilbert Blane, a doctor with such good connections that he was appointed physician of the fleet. Blane knew of the *Treatise* and with the support of his sponsor, the eminent Admiral Sir George Rodney, composed his famous *Memorial to the Admiralty*, recommending the adoption of Lind's cure for scurvy.

Blane's advice was supported by a further trial of lemon juice in 1794 – the year Lind died – in which crewmen on the *Suffolk* were given a daily dose of 2–3 ounces during their passage to India. Not one man fell ill with scurvy during the 23-week voyage – a fact that so impressed the Admiralty it almost immediately ordered every ship to carry ample supplies of citrus fruit as a preventative.[6]

Blane was not an innovator like Lind – a man whose other life-saving ideas included solar stills for making fresh water and the recommendation that every sailor should wear a standard naval uniform that should be kept clean as a guard against typhus.[7] But their roles in the story of scurvy highlight the importance of influential supporters and the fact that innovation is as much a social process as an act of invention: something new is created, it is recognized as an improvement over what already exists, and then it spreads.

Lind and Lancaster may have found that lemon juice was effective against scurvy, but without the Admiralty's recognition their discovery was becalmed. What finally swayed the navy was the endorsement of Lind's ideas by an influential man – Blane – with an even more influential sponsor – Admiral Rodney.

So, in 1795, the most powerful navy on earth finally adopted the cure for scurvy and the devastating malady was wiped out almost overnight. But if it looked like a no-brainer from then on, it obviously wasn't compelling enough for the merchant fleet to embrace it: that took another 70 years.

SANITATION AND WHAT THE ROMANS DID FOR US

If nearly 300 years seems a long time to take up a simple idea that saved thousands of lives, consider the history of plumbing.

Sanitation is arguably one of the greatest innovations in history. The supply of clean water and the hygienic removal of waste have contributed more to the health of the world than any high-tech medicine – even penicillin. But despite its 4,000-year history, sanitation has yet to reach much of the Earth's poorer regions. According to figures produced by the United Nations, 40% of the world's population lacks adequate sanitation and nearly 20% don't even have a decent supply of water that's safe enough to drink.[8] In Asia alone, it is estimated that every year, 500,000 children die from diarrhoea contracted by drinking contaminated water – and we know this because we have an understanding of microbiology.[9]

Back in Roman times, when plumbing engineers built vast sewers and toilets that were emptied with running water, there was no knowledge of the bacteria that caused most life-threatening disease. With no understanding of why Roman plumbing was such an improvement over

---

The greatest innovations of all time?

For what it's worth, here's the author's list (in no particular order) of the greatest innovations ever: plumbing, clothing and footwear, bread, tools and hunting implements, bricks and mortar, glass, money and commerce, healthcare, electricity, the scientific method, wheels, gears, levers, food storage and preservation, writing, motors, typesetting, metal working, flight, democracy and social order, gunpowder, penicillin, mastery of radio waves, TV, navigation and timekeeping, control of fire, lenses, electronics and computers.

what existed before, it's hardly surprising that the Britons ignored it for more than a millennium and got by with bushes or buckets emptied into the street. It wasn't until Victorian times that Britain really cleaned up its act and started building sewers and flushing toilets. What this shows is that innovations must be recognized as such before they can spread.

Apart from sanitation, the Romans who came to Britain brought other innovations, including sophisticated building and engineering techniques, highways, bricks and mortar, breathtaking architecture and under-floor central heating. When the Roman influence finally ebbed away, in the 6th century, these innovations too were largely discarded.

Does it seem rational that, having been exposed to such clever ideas, the Britons should then ignore them for centuries? According to Dr JD Hill, Curator of Iron Age Collections at the British Museum in London, the answer is yes. 'What seems so sensible to us may not have been sensible to them,' he explains of the Britons' preference for simple stone and wooden huts. 'To us it is perfectly normal to live in centrally heated houses, but houses are not simply shelters to keep us warm, they are very much symbols of our lifestyle and culture. The idea of having a permanent house built in brick or stone is tied in with the idea that you're going to be living in the same place for generations.'

Dr Hill points out that only the top echelons of society in Roman Britain could actually afford to live in the villas that archaeologists uncover today. 'Living in a villa with central heating was part and parcel of how aristocrats in Roman Britain lived,' he explains. 'If you change those values to ones that are more to do with being a successful warrior, living in a hall and feasting with your followers, those sorts of houses aren't needed anymore.'

In addition, Britain's economic infrastructure was unlikely to have been able to support the brick-making industry that would have been essential to maintain the Roman innovations in building, so our ancestors made do with stone and wood, wattle and daub, and fires in the middle of the hut.

Another innovation that the Britons ignored – apparently for economic reasons – was the potter's wheel. The unique sales proposition of the potter's wheel is simple: it helps you to make more pots. By any definition, that fulfils the criterion of being 'better than the old method', which was making pots by hand. But according to Dr Hill, the vast majority of pots that the Romans bought from the Brits were handmade.

'The potter's wheel arrived in Britain in about 100BC but people in Northern France had been using it since about 400BC,' he explains of its European heritage. 'It wasn't that people in Britain didn't know about the potter's wheel, because there was ample trade and travel between the two countries.' In fact, says Dr Hill, as early as 100BC, British potters were knocking out handmade copies of stoneware that had been thrown on the wheels of France!

So why did they forego a technology that could help them boost productivity and make a lot more money? 'There must have been deep cultural reasons why it was ignored,' explains Dr Hill of the wheel's apparent failure in Roman Britain. It should have made the potters more productive, but that doesn't seem to have been an issue. Perhaps it was an economic reason, such as being able to guarantee a certain number of orders before investing in the technology, although it was not that expensive to acquire. In fact, says Dr Hill, it was probably a question of scale – the local potters simply didn't need volume production because they were probably peasant farmers who made a small batch of pots every year and sold them to the nearby Romans. In doing this, they might have made enough money to keep them going for another year. The 'old way' suited their needs; it wasn't broken, so why fix it?

WHEN NEW YORK HUMMED TO THE SOUND OF ELECTRIC CARS

If saving lives, more efficient counting and increased profits aren't enough for an innovation to spread like wildfire, how about other benefits like technical superiority or environmental friendliness?

At the end of the 19th century the electric car scored highly on both of these. It was a feature of New York's roads as early as 1897, when fleets of electric taxicabs ferried passengers across the bustling city. At that time, the internal combustion engine was regarded as cranky and unreliable, not to mention noisy and dirty, yet it quickly usurped its rival to become the dominant means of power in the cars we drive today.

By the time the plug was finally pulled on New York's electric cars in 1911, advances in technology had made the internal combustion engine a more viable proposition than its rival. Conventional wisdom holds that the electric car was overtaken because its batteries weren't up to the task. But David Kirsch, a historian who is now a professor of entrepreneurship at the University of Maryland, has challenged such a technologically deterministic view.

Kirsch argues that electric cars were a perfectly adequate technology for getting around town. The problem was that the early adopters wanted to feel the wind in their hair!

'Electric cars didn't fail as a technology, they failed as a value proposition to those early adopters,' he explains of their eventual demise. 'People didn't want what the technology could do, they wanted something quite different.'

According to Kirsch, we drive internal combustion vehicles today because the early adopters were wealthy white men who wanted a high-speed toy for rushing around the countryside. It was a need for which the internal combustion vehicle was uniquely suited, even if the early petrol-engined cars were so unreliable that their owners were often accompanied by mechanics. The electric vehicle, on the other hand, was a perfectly good technology, but it was a utilitarian technology and the early adopters didn't have a utilitarian bent. It was fine for driving 30–40 miles a day across New York, but that was boring. If you were going to fork out thousands of dollars on a plaything, you wanted something with a bit more 'va va voom' than a milk float!

One of the main barriers to the spread of electric cars was the lack of infrastructure in the countryside. The electrification of rural America didn't happen to any great extent until the 1930s, but gasoline had long since been available as a domestic fuel. The internal combustion engine therefore piggybacked on an infrastructure designed to warm people's homes.

Kirsch makes an intriguing point about the *zeitgeist* surrounding electricity at the turn of the 19th century. 'If you look at the history of electrification, the 1880s were about the spread of lighting, the 1890s were about the electrification of horse cars, so everyone expected further advances.'

Here was a 'miracle technology' whose next domain would be the highway. Everyone knew the battery was its weakness, but at the time the attitude was very much 'where there's a will, there's a way' and so everyone

Tucker's amazing automobile

The automotive industry has a rich history of great ideas that flopped, but one of the most famous is the Tucker, a revolutionary saloon car launched in the US in 1947. Described as 'The first really new car in 50 years', the sleek-looking Tucker boasted features that were truly revolutionary for its time. Its engine was a six cylinder, horizontally opposed affair mounted at the rear of the car between the wheels. If that wasn't surprising enough for 1947, it was built from aluminium, water cooled, had a three-speed automatic gear box and was based on a design intended for helicopters. The Tucker's wheels had independent suspension and disk brakes, its interior sported a padded dashboard, upholstery throughout, and a pop-out windscreen for safety. Other safety features included front and rear steel bulkheads and a safety cell for passengers. On its front, the Tucker sported a third headlight, which swivelled as the steering wheel turned.

The Tucker was the brainchild of Preston Tucker, a charismatic car salesman turned innovator whose gut feeling for what customers wanted led him to dream up his audacious design and drive his team to produce it in just ten months.

But Tucker's finance-raising activities attracted the attention of America's Securities and Exchange Commission (SEC), which dogged him with investigations into his sale of franchises and the Tucker Corporation's Initial Public Offering, which raised more than $20 million. Tucker was even charged with conspiracy and fraud, but was acquitted in what was widely regarded as a travesty of a court case.

In an open letter published in several newspapers, Tucker accused his inquisitors of running a dirty tricks campaign at the behest of the automobile industry, which he accused of wanting to bury his innovative design. Having launched his car in 1947, Tucker's company was hit by another SEC investigation, which shattered investor confidence. Production had hardly begun before his factory closed as creditors circled the doomed company. Just 51 cars ever left the factory; most of them are now in museums – a lasting tribute to an automotive innovation that failed. Years later, many of Tucker's ideas were picked up by rival motor manufacturers – the industry he claimed had set out to crush him.

expected a breakthrough that would make it happen. In fact, it was the internal combustion engine that advanced in leaps and bounds and by 1910 it was competing on a battleground that was dramatically different from ten years before.[10]

THE FAILURE OF BRUNEL'S VISIONARY RAILWAY

Another innovative transportation technology that bombed was the 'atmospheric railway' built in south Devon by Isambard Kingdom Brunel, arguably the greatest engineer that ever lived. For a while in the 1840s, Britain's railway engineers flirted with the idea of an 'atmospheric railway' that would overcome some of the perceived shortcomings of steam engines. Although steam locomotives had proven themselves more than a decade earlier, doubts still persisted about their ability to climb hills or maintain high speeds on longer routes.[11]

In short, the atmospheric system would use compressed air from engine houses along the track to push the train which, having no need for an engine or fuel, would be lighter and quicker than its rival. The propulsion came from air pushing against a piston enclosed in a tube between the rails. An iron rod connected the piston to the train above it and the whole affair moved when the compressed air was turned on. Trials in London enjoyed a degree of initial success and in the heady days of railway mania, Brunel got the go-ahead to build 20 miles of track from Exeter to Newton Abbot, a section of which ran along the coast near Teignmouth. Work began in 1844 and part of the line opened in 1847, with the rest being completed the following year. But on 5 September 1848, the atmospheric railway gasped its last breath and the system was shut down.

What had gone wrong? The main cause of failure was technological. Because the train and the piston were joined by a metal rod, the pipe providing the compressed air could not be sealed effectively enough for the system to work properly. Along its length it needed a valve that would open and shut when the train and its rod came along. Unfortunately, with the materials available at the time, it was simply not possible to do this. Part of the valve was leather, which decayed in the rain and sea spray, and the wax that was applied to keep it supple attracted the attention of hungry rats. Without a properly sealed pipe, the compressed air leaked out and the whole affair was rendered useless.

But although it was primarily a failure of technology, other factors contributed to the demise of the atmospheric railway:

- The concept was given a chance because the embryonic railway industry was experiencing an investment boom, so any plausible idea could find funding in the uncertainty, hype and mania that existed. Brunel's support only added credibility to the idea. In 1847 the railway boom went bust and the funding dried up, so it's unlikely that new funding could have been raised to sort out all the problems.
- As with electric cars, it seems everyone underestimated the rival technology of steam, which quickly proved it was more than up to the task.
- Although initial trials of the atmospheric system had proved encouraging, the technology was still unproven. Despite this lack of technological validation, Brunel went ahead anyway. In addition, the effects of sea spray and rain on the leather should have been anticipated.
- Sometimes, visionaries make mistakes. Although Brunel was certainly a brilliant engineer, he was not an expert on steam and was therefore more amenable to alternative ways of thinking. However, both George and Robert Stephenson – the pioneers of the steam train – had expressed their doubts about the system after seeing the trials in London. Their opinions were ignored – possibly because they were not experts on atmospheric railways!

In principle, the idea of separating the motive power from the train itself was sound. It just turned out that electricity, not air, was the way it would later be achieved – at the expense of steam locomotion.

SO YOU THINK YOU'LL CHANGE THE WORLD?

Looking back at all of these examples, it's clear that the history of innovation is littered with the debris of great ideas that flopped. Cultural resistance, apathy, economics, hype, vested interests, ignoring feedback from others and a lack of forethought all had a part to play. As we'll find out later on, they still do.

More compelling innovations than the metric system or internet shopping have yet to achieve widespread, let alone universal, adoption – so if you think your big idea is going to change the world, think again!

Consider what innovations are available to everyone on the planet – and I mean absolutely everyone. The list is hardly extensive: clothing and footwear, bread, shelter, basic cooking and hunting tools, control of fire, rudimentary agriculture and healthcare. Innovations like these have been around for thousands of years. What's more, they're simple to implement, affordable and don't require an infrastructure.

Now look at the National Academy of Engineering's 'Greatest Engineering Achievements of the 20th Century'[12]:

1. Electrification	11. Highways
2. The automobile	12. Spacecraft
3. Air travel	13. The internet
4. Water supply and distribution	14. Imaging
5. Electronics	15. Household appliances
6. Radio and TV	16. Health technologies
7. Agricultural mechanization	17. Petrochemicals
8. Computers	18. Lasers and fibre optics
9. Telephones	19. Nuclear technologies
10. Air conditioning and refrigeration	20. High-performance materials

How long will it be before any of these are available to 100% of the world's population? Probably never, in most cases. More than 125 years after its invention, the telephone is nothing like ubiquitous; most people have never flown, electrification is beyond the reach of many remote areas and even rudimentary sanitation and basic personal hygiene have yet to make inroads into much of Africa and Asia.

It's important to understand that people are not rational adopters of innovations simply because they are cheaper, better, easier to use, more convenient or even life-saving. If that was the case we'd all be teleworking from home and shopping online at WebVan; the roads would hum with electric cars and AIDS would never have spread.

So, if ever you hear a 'visionary' futurist spouting on about how the internet will transform the lives of everybody on the planet, just think about sanitation and tell them they're talking crap!

New Coke – how innovation almost killed an American icon
Product innovations sometimes involve tweaking the existing line to create a 'new and improved' version – known as a 'reformulation'. But the outcry that followed the introduction of New Coke in 1985 shows that some products shouldn't be tampered with, even if the reasons for doing so seem compelling. Coke, with its familiar, 99-year old taste, was the most successful product in history. In fact, it had become more than just a product – it was a symbol of a nation, as much as the Star Spangled Banner and baseball. Across the world – particularly in communist countries – it was a symbol of freedom and aspiration, not just a drink.

But in the early 1980s it was losing market share to Pepsi, whose 'Pepsi Challenge' was highlighting the fact that drinkers actually preferred the taste of Pepsi in blind tests. Coca-Cola tested the market and asked people what they might think of a reformulation, but the response they got was discouraging. However, in late 1984, Coca-Cola's researchers developed a new, sweeter tasting Coke that beat Pepsi time after time in blind tastings. Extensive market research showed that the new formula could be introduced into the market in place of the old, but it would lose around 12% of Coke's existing customers. What they didn't reckon with was the fact that those loyal Coke drinkers would cause an outcry when the new formulation was introduced in April 1985, especially when people realized that a piece of American history was about to be phased out. The backlash gained momentum in the media and within three months Coke was forced to do a U-turn and reintroduce the familiar old taste that people knew and loved and which they apparently took for granted. The idea that Coke might disappear reminded people what it was they liked about it and so they started buying it again. Over the next few months, sales of Coke and Coca-Cola's share price began to rise, and all because of a marketing innovation that failed!

British Airways – not flying the flag

Business decisions can be as innovative as launching new products – and they can be just as risky, too. British Airways took the bold step of re-branding its corporate image in 1997 to reflect its status and aspirations as a truly worldwide airline. In a £60 million revamp, the carrier's traditional red, white and blue tail fin design – which reflected the national flag – was replaced by 50 different designs based on arts and crafts from around the world. Jets were repainted with images such as calligraphy, African art and the tartans of Scotland. This new international flavour followed what BA's [then] chief executive, Bob Ayling, claimed was probably the largest exercise in market research ever undertaken by an airline. But the bold re-branding immediately came under fire and hit the headlines later in the year when former Prime Minister Margaret Thatcher famously draped a handkerchief over a model airliner sporting one of the new designs. Although 60% of BA's passengers were from outside the UK, the unfortunate fact was that the other 40% were from Britain and it was their dislike of the more cosmopolitan tail fins – along with some snide reporting in the media – that eventually sealed their fate. Two years later, BA announced it would drop its world images and replace them with a new design that once again reflected the national flag. As Coca-Cola found out when it introduced New Coke, it seems that innovators take their lives in their hands when they decide to mess around with potent national symbols.

NOTES

1 *Harvard Business Review*, November 1989.

2 13.75p actually, but we rounded up, much to the delight of the shop-keepers.

3 *The Latex Condom: Recent advances, future directions.* Family Health International (www.fhi.org).

4 *The Latex Condom*, Chapter 2.

5 James Lind, *A Treatise of the Scurvy*, 1753.

6 Apart from oranges and lemons, the ships also carried limes, which is why Americans call the Brits 'limeys'.

7 Source: *Handbook for Royal Navy Medical Officers*, published by the Royal Navy. Lind also recommended that surgeons wash their hands between examining patients and he noticed a connection between tropical fevers and insects.

8 *Progress made in Providing Safe Water Supply and Sanitation for all during the 1990s*; Report of the Secretary General, United Nations, 2000. It defines adequate sanitation as a system that hygienically separates human waste from human contact, and it includes simple covered pit latrines. Considered unsafe are buckets, open pit latrines and going behind a bush.

9 *Freshwater: A global crisis of water security and basic water provision*; Environment Briefing No.1, published by Towards Earth Summit 2002.

10 Kirsch has written an excellent book on the subject: *The Electric Vehicle and the Burden of History*. Rutgers University Press, 2000.

11 The failure of the atmospheric railway is documented by RA Buchanan in a paper entitled *The Atmospheric Railway of IK Brunel*. It appears in *Social Studies of Science*, Vol. 22, 1992 – an edition devoted to failed innovations.

12 www.greatachievements.org

3

Flowers and weeds

'There are no bad ideas or bad products or bad innovations,
just bad applications for them and bad contexts.'

Nick Jankel-Elliott
Director of Strategy, Happy Dog Group

Having read the previous two chapters you're probably screaming: 'But those innovations didn't fail, they just went away for a while' – and you'd be right. You'd also be right to point out that innovations like sanitation and the metric system are hugely successful in some countries and struggling elsewhere. What this highlights about innovation is that success and failure are very much functions of time, space and perception.

WHAT IS INNOVATION?

In his book *Diffusion of Innovations*, Everett Rogers argues that innovation is a social and temporal process involving four key elements: 'the innovation', which is spread through 'communication channels' over a period of 'time' to the members of a 'social system'.

Rogers defines an innovation as:

'An idea, practice or object that is perceived as new by an individual or other unit of adoption.'

It's an elegant definition that recognizes the fact that the innovation is in the eye of the beholder. It also recognizes that innovations don't necessarily have to be the products of technological development. In fact, many studies of innovation in the US have focused on new teaching methods in schools.

Another elegant definition comes from Bob Metcalfe, one of the pioneers of computer networking. In the November 1999 issue of *MIT Technology Review* he wrote:

'Invention is a flower, innovation is a weed.'

Metcalfe's point is that invention is not enough; like a weed, the innovation must spread and survive – it must 'diffuse'.

Drawing on another botanical analogy, it seems that many innovations are like spores: they germinate and grow, but fail to flourish because conditions aren't right, so they enter a dormant phase and come back to life when conditions are right. The electric car is a good example, as are the efforts to launch satellites from balloons – an idea that was first tried in the mid-1950s, and then again at the turn of the 21st century.

Schumpeter's trilogy and the nature of technical change

The economist Josef Schumpeter devised a 'trilogy' to explain the nature of innovation and technical change. First, there is 'invention', which encompasses the creation of new ideas, often in the research laboratory. Then comes 'innovation', which is the process of commercializing (or popularizing) those ideas into a proposition that consumers (or users) will find attractive. In some cases, innovation will result from the combination of existing technologies or processes into something new. The final part of the trilogy is the 'diffusion' of innovations into the market or into society as a whole. At each stage there are selective forces at work: an invention might not be developed, an innovation might not be adopted by the market.

Academics and consultants have come up with many other notions of innovation, some more outlandish than others. Type the words 'innovation' and 'definition' into a search engine and you'll find the following ideas:

> 'Innovation is invention plus exploitation,'
> 'Innovation is the ability to deliver new value to a customer,'

and

> 'Innovation is a process, involving multiple activities, performed by multiple actors from one or several organizations, during which new combinations of means and/or ends, which are new for a creating and/or adopting unit, are developed and/or produced and/or implemented and/or transferred to old and/or new market partners.'[1]

Phew!

But innovation is more than just creating and launching new products. Innovations can be:

- **services**, like search engines or price comparison systems on the internet
- **ideas**, eg 'the earth orbits the sun' or 'man evolved from the apes'
- **ideologies**, such as democracy, capitalism, communism
- **social innovations**, including public health, welfare, new types of sport
- **processes**, such as total quality management or new methods of teaching
- **business strategies**, for example launching a company or merging with another.

For most readers, the experience of innovation will be an invention, a product launch or a new business. The success or failure of each will be influenced by the same factors: the inherent characteristics of the innovation; the environment in which it is created; the infrastructure that allows it to flourish; the characteristics of potential adopters and their perception of the innovation itself. As we'll see in Chapter 6, the characteristics of innovators also have an important bearing on the success or failure of their innovations.

THE CHARACTERISTICS OF INNOVATIONS

In Chapter 1 we looked at five characteristics that Everett Rogers argued would determine the success or failure of innovations: relative advantage, compatibility, complexity, trialability and observability.

Other researchers have expanded the list to include the following:[2]

- **Risk:** Are there risks in buying or using it, or does it reduce some kind of risk?
- **Discretion:** Does it deny the user the ability to make choices of their own? For example, online grocery stores deny people the chance to pick their own fruit.
- **Image:** Does it harm or enhance the user's image? What does this signal about the user to others?
- **Capability:** Can it do the job sufficiently? Think of an MP3 player with only five minutes of storage!
- **Similarity/differentiation:** Users will be less likely to adopt an innovation if they have had a bad experience with something similar. They will be more likely to adopt it if they feel it offers a much better experience than whatever already exists.
- **Divisibility:** Whereas trialability might be downloading an evaluation copy of software, divisibility is more like trying a single-user licence before buying a site licence.
- **Adopting or switching costs:** The extent to which adopting the innovation requires investment in money and time – think of new IT systems.
- **Cost/benefits:** The benefits gained for the investment required. For example, you might receive an electronic coupon via your mobile phone, offering you 20% off a cappuccino at a coffee shop half a mile away. Is it really worth the effort of walking there to cash it in?

- **Network effects:** The more phones there are, the greater the value of the phone system.
- **Interoperability:** The degree to which the innovation can interact with complementary products, eg video playback software such as RealPlayer and QuickTime, which work with a variety of browsers.
- **Co-dependence:** Does the innovation rely on something else? For example, the Anoto wireless digital pen (see Chapter 10) requires specially printed paper to work. Mobile internet devices require small screens.
- **Standards:** Does the innovation create or challenge a standard? If a standard exists, how large is its installed base?
- **Build and reliability:** Can it be built cheaply and maintained easily? A hotel in space is certainly an innovative idea; building it is another matter!
- **Disposability:** Is disposal easy and cheap? Not if it's a nuclear power station!
- **Inducements and subsidies:** Is the innovation subsidized to increase the rate of uptake? Think of mobile phones – cheaper with a contract.

All of these characteristics together form a proposition, and it's the adopter's *perception* of the proposition that counts, not the innovation itself.

WHAT'S NEW?

Looking back at Everett Rogers' definition of innovation, he also makes the point that an innovation needn't necessarily be new. This is certainly the case with most 'new' products – in reality, very few of them are either innovative or new.

An interesting definition of 'newness' comes from *New Product Management in the 1980s*, a classic study of innovation published in 1982 by the management consultancy Booz Allen & Hamilton. Surveying 13,000 'new' products introduced by 700 companies between 1976 and 1981, they identified six shades of newness:

- new to the world **10%**
- new to the company, allowing it to enter an existing market **20%**

- line extensions   **26%**
- improvements or revisions   **26%**
- product repositionings   **7%**
- cost reductions   **11%**

So 90% of 'new' products are actually rejigs, tweaks or 'me too' lines, not new and innovative products designed to push the envelope.

Looking at supermarket goods – one of the biggest markets for new product introductions – more recent studies have found even less innovation. According to Productscan® Online, which has spent 20 years monitoring all new launches of food, beverage, health and beauty, household and pet products in the supermarkets of North America, a record 32,025 new lines hit the shelves in 2001. But how many of these were truly innovative?

To qualify as innovative and score on Productscan's 'Innovation Rating', new products must satisfy at least one of the following six criteria:

- **new positioning** to reach new users or new ways of use
- providing a new customer benefit through **new packaging**
- introducing a **new formulation**
- adding **new technology** to the product
- opening a **new market** for the product
- **new merchandizing** methods to sell the product.

Productscan found that just 7% of 'new' products launched in 2001 earned their Innovation Rating – and that was a good year. In 2000, it was 6.6%. Here again, more than 90% of launches are line extensions, tweaks or 'me too' products.

Examples of innovative products identified by Productscan in 2001 include: 'Campbell's Soup to Sip' microwaveable soup, which comes in a carton with a sip-through lid; 'Parkay Fun Squeeze Colored Margarine', which allows kids to cover their bread with gooey graffiti; a colour-changing nail varnish; and 'Guinness Draught' in bottles.

How many of these innovative products will become durable brands? The odds of surviving are not good, according to Productscan's Tom Vierhile: 'The ballpark figure everyone uses is an 80% failure rate for new products,' he says of the household products and food market. The numbers are depressingly persuasive: the average supermarket carries 30–40,000 lines, but 32,025 new products were launched in 2001 alone. As Vierhile notes: 'Maybe some of those new products shouldn't be coming to market.'

THE CLIMATE OF CHANGE

The characteristics of innovations are like the genes of a weed – they equip it for certain conditions, but these can't be guaranteed. Even weeds will shrivel and die if the climate is too harsh. For innovations, there are several environmental factors that will determine success or failure.

Firstly, there has to be a supportive climate within the company so that new ideas can thrive. If good ideas and creative minds are discouraged, innovation will not flourish – as most books on the subject will tell you. If a company has an isolated, autocratic boss, bad ideas can be waved through, and good ideas binned. Then there are issues of funding, as most dotcom innovators found to their cost. If the climate goes from boom to bust, even good ideas will find it hard to secure funding. What about the wider economy? Will people go out and spend money on whatever it is you're developing? Everybody tightens their belts in a recession.

In many cases, innovations can be 'pushed' by technological developments rather than 'pulled' by market demand. The World Wide Web wasn't driven by demand, nor was Napster, the music and file sharing system. Both were developed by people who saw the technical possibilities and thought there was a market for what they were creating.

So innovation is a combination of foresight and opportunism – the ability to see where an innovation might fit into an environment that is constantly changing. It's also about looking into the future and seeing periods of stability that will allow an innovation to grab a niche and then stay there.

In this way, the disruptive nature of innovation is rather like the evolutionary theory of Punctuated Equilibrium – there are periods of sudden upheaval in which many new forms are given a chance, followed by a much longer period of calm in which most fade away and die, leaving a few successful forms to thrive.

For the success of an innovation such as MP3, both upheaval and stability are necessary. The upheaval was the birth of the internet, advances in file compression, disk space and file sharing, and the development of pocket-sized players as solid state memory got cheaper and hard disks got smaller. There was also a change in people's attitude towards the ownership and enjoyment of music. From having a CD collection that was both tangible and visible and played on a machine that was designed for playing music, people are now beginning to regard music as being more like software – intangible and to be used on a computer. All of these factors came together to allow MP3 to grab its market niche.

But now that it has found that niche, MP3 needs a long period of stability in order to flourish; just think where we'd be if new file formats came along every week! Like VHS before it, MP3 didn't need to be the best technology to dominate its niche, but having proved itself a survivor, its initial success will be reinforced in this period of calm as manufacturers and consumers turn it into an industry standard.

Another factor crucial to the success of innovation is the communications infrastructure that enables its spread. Napster, for example, went from zero to hero in a matter of months because it was free and easily downloaded over the internet. This, in turn, contributed to the success of MP3. Napster was unusual in the sense that its success didn't rely on mass marketing, such as advertising or publicity. Its incredible rise was more down to word of mouth and favourable press coverage. We'll look at the downside of hyping innovation in Chapter 5.

Although mass media are important for influencing a large number of people to adopt an innovation, the success of Napster shows that word of mouth can be crucially persuasive as well. But this requires a certain degree of asymmetry: one person must have experience and knowledge of the innovation, the other must be seeking it. If the asymmetry is too great, effective communication of the innovation's benefits may be difficult: imagine a Western professor of medicine describing the principles of virology to peasant farmers in Africa – it's hardly likely to encourage the use of condoms, is it? But if the asymmetry is less marked – for example, the 'change agent' is a local healthcare worker or a respected friend – the effort is likely to be more successful.

THE CHARACTERISTICS OF ADOPTERS

Not all people are born equal when it comes to trying out new ideas. Some of us are enthusiastic and adventurous; others are conservative and cautious. Notice the pro-innovation bias creeping into the language again – something we'll explore in Chapter 5 when we look at hype.

Rogers identified five categories of adopter, based on their willingness to try out new ideas:

- **Innovators:** Making up just 2.5% of the population, the innovators are cosmopolitan, affluent, technologically savvy, educated, daring and open to risky new ideas. They delight in being the first to try out something new, embrace high degrees of uncertainty and technical imperfection and can cope with the fact that the innovation might either bomb or succeed and drop its price dramatically later. These are the geeks who download 'early beta' software.
- **Early adopters:** The next 13.5% of the population, early adopters are also cosmopolitan in their outlook but are far more respected by their peers than the innovators. For this reason, they are 'opinion leaders' – the group with the most influence on later adopters. By adopting and using innovations, early adopters remove much of the fear and uncertainty for everyone else. They buy Version 1.0 software when it's launched.
- **Early majority:** Adopting innovations earlier than most, the early majority are a less adventurous group making up 34% of the total. Neither opinion leaders nor laggards, they will wait until the innovation has been tried and tested by others and they can see the benefits.
- **Late majority:** Another 34% of adopters, who wait even longer to try out a new idea. They are risk-averse, cautious and often sceptical, not affluent and conscious of social norms. Half the entire social group will have adopted an innovation before the late majority embraces it.

● **Laggards:** Parochial and insular, the laggards make up the most conservative 16% of the social system, being suspicious of new ideas and resistant to change.

Remember that these categories apply as much to companies and organizations as they do to people. As adopters come round to accepting the innovation, a graph plotting adoption against time will take on a characteristic S-curve (see below). Rogers estimates that the take-off point happens when 10–25% of the group has embraced the innovation, confirming the important influence of the early adopters.

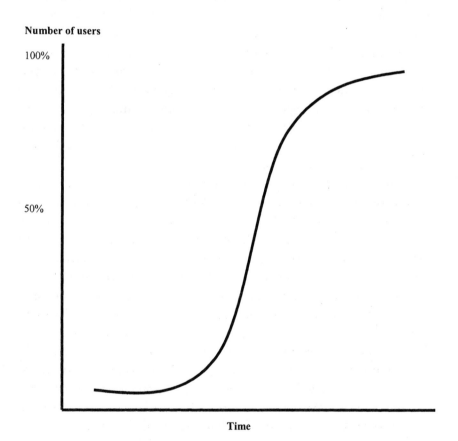

Number of users

100%

50%

Time

Earlier adopters are usually more affluent, educated, cosmopolitan, adventurous and enjoy a higher status than later adopters. In the corporate world, they are likely to be the larger, more affluent companies or organizations.

There are many exceptions, however. When satellite television came to the UK its early adopters were among the less affluent members of society. In business, smaller companies are, by virtue of their size, more able to deploy new information technologies – as long as their budgets permit.

Remember that people and organizations will differ in the rate at which they adopt different innovations. The wirehead in technical support may be an innovator when it comes to the latest mobile phone, but a laggard when it comes to the newest personal hygiene products. This illustrates what academics call the 'innovative needs paradox' – that the people who most need an innovation are usually the last to adopt it!

For all of these groups, the decision to adopt an innovation is a process that begins with the **knowledge** that the innovation exists and the **recognition** that it solves a problem or fulfils a need. Next comes an **opinion-forming** stage that often relies on the influence of other people. The **decision to adopt** is followed by **implementation** and finally **retention** and **confirmation** that the decision has been correct.

HOW DO YOU DEFINE SUCCESS OR FAILURE?

The fact that the decision process ends with retention and confirmation rather than adoption, highlights the fact that successful innovation is about much more than simply shifting products or getting someone to run with a new idea. How many products have you gone out and bought, only to neglect or even discard them after the novelty has worn off? (Include that gym membership you never use!)

So how do we define success? Meeting sales targets? Market share? Customer satisfaction? Technical excellence? Return on investment? Lives saved or disease prevented?

And in what time frame should we measure it? Remember that many – if not most – innovations eventually come good, sometimes after centuries.

One interesting attempt to quantify new product success is the Success Measurement Project, sponsored by the Product Development and Management Association in the US.

The authors, Abbie Griffin and Albert Page, extended the work of Booz Allen & Hamilton by using the same six product criteria we encountered earlier in the chapter. Based on a survey of 80 product development specialists, they devised ten benchmarks against which to judge the success or failure of new products. As shown in the table below, they found that a combination of criteria could be used, depending on the product strategy, or its 'newness'.

Success criteria	Newness of product					
	New to world	New to company	Line extensions	Improvements	Repositioning	Cost reductions
Customer acceptance	✓		✓		✓	✓
Customer satisfaction	✓	✓	✓	✓	✓	✓
Competitive advantage	✓	✓	✓	✓	✓	
Met profit goals	✓	✓	✓	✓	✓	
Return on investment	✓					
Met market share goals		✓	✓	✓	✓	
Met revenue goals		✓		✓		✓
Met margin goals						✓
Performance specifications						✓
Quality specifications						✓

Source: PDMA Success Measurement Project: Recommended measures for product development success and failure. *Journal of Product Innovation Management*, 1996; 13: 478–496.

With any innovation, both the adopter and the innovator have their own ideas of success and failure, but who is to judge? Let's consider some examples:

- Internet Explorer cost millions to develop and Microsoft gives it away.
- MacOS is widely regarded as being technically superior to Windows and a lot easier to use, yet it enjoys less than 7% market share because PCs are cheaper than AppleMacs and offer a wider range of software.
- *Blade Runner* bombed at the box office and the critics panned it. Twenty years on, it's regarded as one of the finest films ever made.
- Stephen Hawking's book *A Brief History of Time* was a publishing sensation; but do you know anyone who has actually read it?
- Xerox invented the mouse and the graphical interface, Apple made them popular and Microsoft made them ubiquitous.
- Concorde was a technological marvel that everyone wanted to fly but nobody wanted to buy.
- The plan to replace Classic Coke with New Coke back in 1985 was a marketing fiasco that boosted the price of Coca-Cola shares.
- The US isn't metric, everyone else is. Everyone else uses GSM phones as well.
- Napster was so successful it was banned and the company behind it failed.

What these examples illustrate is that social innovations, new technologies and new products don't pass through some rational form of assessment in which adopters make logical decisions based on objective scientific evidence, so that only the 'best' innovations or technologies survive.

Such a view of the world is naïve. It ignores the quirky, irrational, apathetic and often capricious nature of human decision-making, just as it ignores the questions of 'best for whom, by what criteria, in what time frame and at what cost?' Moreover, it ignores our unfailing ability to ask of innovation the toughest question of all: 'So what?'

Unfortunately, many innovators *are* naïve – particularly those working in high technology and the internet. They believe that people will use a technology simply because it exists or because it is technologically superior to something else; they believe that people will buy something because they're offered a lower price, or because they can order it online; they believe that everyone wants to be connected to the internet, 24 hours a day.

From this naïve world view come innovations that are destined to fail, no matter how brilliant they are.

Oops ... that wasn't supposed to happen

Innovators may start out with an honest intention to improve mankind's lot, but many successful and beneficial innovations have unintended and unforeseen consequences that create problems of their own. Here are a few examples:

- **The motor car:** Millions killed and injured in road accidents, pollution, the breakdown of communities, increased crime, health problems including respiratory diseases and obesity, gridlocked streets that reduce mobility. (Ironically, if you produced a cheap, safe, non-polluting car that ran on water, gridlock would get far worse!)
- **The internet:** Spread of child pornography, copyright theft, loss of productivity because people surf in office time, identity theft, hacking, computer crime.
- **Email:** Viruses, marketing spam, productivity lost through dealing with unnecessary communications, increased workload resulting in higher stress.
- **Computers:** Increased workload, increased use of paper, spiralling costs of upgrading hardware and software, hacking and computer security, the Millennium Bug.
- **Television:** Breakdown of family communication, obesity, reality TV.
- **Mobile phones:** Increase in street robberies in the UK.
- **International travel:** More rapid spread of disease across continents, the spread of ecologically damaging alien species, the spread of drugs, destruction of pristine environments.
- **Ready meals and junk food:** Loss of basic cooking skills, poor diet and health problems such as obesity and diabetes.
- **Antibiotics:** Antibiotic resistant pathogens.

Should unforeseen and unintended consequences be factored into the assessment of whether an innovation has succeeded or failed? Don't forget that many innovations have unforeseen consequences that are positively beneficial to society, often because they are combined with other technologies to create new innovations. Lasers, for example, weren't invented to play music or films. Viagra was originally tested for heart conditions. Some innovations are reinvented by users – for example, Apple's iPod was 'hacked' so that users could store their address books on it! Apple later incorporated the hack into its iPod software.

IDEAS FOR INNOVATORS

- Just because it's a great idea, it doesn't mean people will use it. It has to be a great proposition, pitched at the right time to the right market. Context is everything if innovation is to succeed.
- Think up your own definition of innovation.
- Look back at the characteristics of innovations earlier in the chapter and see how your own innovation scores on each.
- Describe a typical adopter from each group.
- How will you attract each group of users, from 'innovators' to 'laggards'? Don't assume you've produced something so good it will sell itself.
- How will your innovation evolve so that each group feels comfortable adopting it?
- What is the adoption decision process for your innovation? How could you improve your chances at each step?
- How will you define success? Will you change the goal posts?
- How will people reinvent your innovation?
- What will be the unintended consequences of your innovation? All innovations have them, so try to think of at least three.

NOTES

1 These definitions were all on the same website: www.innovation.cc/discussion_papers/definition.htm.

2 The source of most of these characteristics is a remarkably insightful document produced by America's Federal Highways Agency in 1996 entitled *Development of Human Factors Guidelines for Advanced Traveler Information Systems and Commercial Vehicle Operations – Exploring driver acceptance of in-vehicle information systems.* FHWA-RD-96–143.

4

Learning the lessons of the past

'Learn from the mistakes of others.
You can't live long enough to make them all yourself.'

Anonymous

INTRODUCTION

There's a famous saying that those who don't learn the lessons of history are doomed to repeat the mistakes of the past. Unfortunately, it seems that failure is one thing that many entrepreneurs would rather not think about, just as dotcom investors ignored the lessons of history and told the rest of us: 'It's different this time'. As the playwright Lillian Hellman once wrote:

> 'It is considered unhealthy in America to remember mistakes, neurotic to think about them, psychotic to dwell on them.'

In the previous chapter we saw Everett Rogers' list of the attributes most likely to determine the success or failure of any innovation. Many of these factors came from studying the diffusion of what could be called 'social' innovations – for example, the introduction of hybrid corn seed in Iowa or the development of new ways to teach mathematics in schools. Indeed, one of the most famous studies of a failed innovation concerns a Peruvian village in which health workers tried to encourage families to boil water before they drank it, in order to destroy harmful bacteria. Their efforts were in vain until they realized that the villagers had no real understanding of microbiology and regarded boiled water as something that was drunk only by people who were *already* sick. Furthermore, the few people who *did* boil water to sterilize it were regarded as outsiders whose behaviour was contrary to the accepted wisdom of the community.

In the realm of business, there are few specific studies of why innovations fail, but many insights can be gleaned from studies of product development.

BOOZ ALLEN & HAMILTON'S NEW PRODUCT MANAGEMENT FOR THE 1980S

Published in 1982, this is still considered something of a classic study of new product development, having surveyed 13,000 launches from 700 industrial companies in the years from 1976 to 1981. On the subject of product failure its key findings were as follows:

- Only 14% of new product ideas generated by companies made it to market.
- The success rate of new products that reached the market was 65%.
- That means that around 91% of new product ideas failed, either before they got to market or in the market itself.
- Forty six per cent of total spending on new product development was lost on failures.
- Companies with a strong track record of successful launches considered fewer ideas for each new product successfully launched.
- The main factor in the success of a new product was its fit with market needs. Technical superiority was considered the third most important factor, after the product's fit with the company's internal strengths.

CALANTONE AND COOPER'S 1979 STUDY OF PRODUCT FAILURE

In 1979, Roger Calantone and Robert Cooper published a study on product failure in the *Journal of the Academy of Marketing Science* which looked at the characteristics of around 200 new products that had failed in the market.

They found that:

- 28% were 'better mousetraps' that nobody wanted
- 24% were 'me too' products that offered little differentiation from rivals
- 15% were technical dogs that didn't work properly
- 13% failed because of price cuts by competitors
- 13% were too expensive for most consumers
- 7% failed because of 'plain and simple ignorance'.

Looking at these reasons more closely, it seems that all but the 'technical dogs' suffered from a more fundamental problem – bad thinking. Companies were launching products with little understanding of the customer or the competitive environment.

Similar findings were reported by Edwin Bobrow and Dennis Shafer in their 1987 book *Pioneering New Products: A market survival guide*, in which they observed a failure rate of around 48% for new products. The main culprits were 'the innovative mousetrap that really wasn't better', which accounted for around a fifth of all failures, and 'me too' products of one kind or another, which made up slightly more.

The failure of innovators to understand the market was highlighted in further studies undertaken by Robert Cooper, which are reported in his book *Winning at New Products*. In one study, published in 1986, Cooper and his colleagues looked at 203 new product launches, of which 123 were successful and 80 failed – a success rate of 61%. The research identified 13 'key activities' in the new product process, from initial screening to market launch. Just 1.9% of all projects included all 13 key activities; the most notable oversight was the detailed market study, which was omitted in 75% of the 203 product launches. Cooper suggests that a good market study should include a study of competitive products and prices, an assessment of customer needs and wants, and an estimate of the market size. In his book, Cooper observes that 'a lack of market information remains the number one cause of product failure.'

It's worth noting that the book was published in 2001 – 22 years after Cooper and Calantone's study of product failure – which means that innovators are obviously still making the same mistakes when they bring new products to market.

NEIL RACKHAM'S STUDY OF SALES TECHNIQUES

In his book *SPIN® Selling*, marketing expert Neil Rackham challenges two common beliefs about new products – that consumers are reluctant to buy them and that sales people are reluctant to sell them. On the contrary, he observes, both are enthusiastic about innovation, but their enthusiasm wanes after the initial excitement. Sales drop off and the sales force becomes disheartened. At this point, sales begin to creep up again.

To understand why, Rackham and his colleagues listened in to 35,000 sales calls made to pitch three new products and recorded 116 different behaviours exhibited by sales people during their conversations. They found the following:

- The more questions sales people asked customers, the more successful they were in selling the product.
- When sales people pitched new products they asked 40% fewer questions. This was because they were spending more time enthusing about new product features.
- The more features they described, the fewer sales they made!

Indeed, Rackham found that focusing on new features was a sales strategy that actually backfired during follow-up calls, ensuring that potential customers quickly lost interest in the product. This, in turn, caused disillusion among sales staff who lost interest in the product and its features. At this point, Rackham contends, they began to push the features less and customers began to take more notice, so sales began to climb!

Rackham concluded that there was a 'fundamental problem' with the way innovative new products were being sold:

'The more innovative the product (and the richer it is in bells and whistles), the more likely sales people will sell it through features rather than through questions. In other words, a powerful new product is likely to make sales people product-centred instead of customer-centred.'

He blames this on the way the companies themselves communicate the product to their sales staff; they emphasize the cool new features, not how the product can make life easier for the consumer.

What the gurus say: Don Norman

Don Norman is one of the most eloquent writers on the design and use of technology. In books such as *The Design of Everyday Things* and *The Invisible Computer*, he argues for human-centred design that focuses on the needs of the user, not on how many 'cool new features' the engineers can pack into the latest product. Though not an empirical study, Norman's observations are worth including because he has spent so much time considering how objects are designed and how they are used in the real world.

In *The Invisible Computer* he offers the following insights:

Good products can fail if:
- they are easy to use but are based on poor technology or lack the capability to do the job
- they are based on great technology and offer significant benefits, but are difficult to use
- they are based on great technology and offer significant benefits, but are too expensive.

Bad products can succeed if:
- they are good enough for consumers' needs
- they are cheaper than more technologically sophisticated rivals
- they have better marketing
- they offer a better value proposition for the customer.

THE BATHWICK GROUP STUDY OF DOTCOM FAILURES

In November 2001, the London-based research consultancy Bathwick Group published a study into the failure of 100 internet companies that collapsed between November 2000 and October 2001. Called *Dotcom Performance: Why they failed*, the study revealed that the top ten internet failures in the UK went under despite having raised £520 million in funding.

The author, Dudley Hawes, found 13 primary causes of business failure, which he grouped into three categories: management, money and markets. But again, one factor emerged above all others: bad thinking.

The report concluded:

'A significant number of dotcoms never had a viable business model and were being funded despite their poor revenues and customer models.'

In addition, the research confirmed Cooper's findings, mentioned earlier, about the lack of proper market analysis. It says:

'Very few of the dotcom companies we examined had bothered to conduct sufficient market research before launching.'

But the most astonishing finding of the research was that an incredible 60% of dotcom entrepreneurs questioned by the Bathwick Group said that online companies offered 'no clear attraction for consumers over offline competition'.

I'll repeat that just in case it didn't sink in the first time:

Most Dotcom entrepreneurs admitted that online companies offered no clear attraction for consumers over offline competition.

Remember that these were the same entrepreneurs who previously had been swigging champagne at First Tuesday meetings and laughing at how they were going to change the world because all those old economy dinosaurs just didn't get it. Today the world looks a whole lot different. Unlike most dotcom start-ups, those old economy dinosaurs are still in business!

According to the Bathwick Group, the 13 primary causes of internet business failure were:

Management failure
- viability of business models
- weak and inexperienced management
- poor organization and execution
- poor customer service
- lack of contingency planning.

Money failure
- poor cost control
- excessive cash burn
- limited revenue streams
- poor funding environment after the bubble burst.

Market failure
- little or no competitive advantage
- failure to define or understand the value proposition for the customer
- failure to understand the value of alliances
- uncertainty over future prospects.

On the inability of most dotcoms to find additional funding, the report concluded:

> 'Many dotcoms failed because they never really warranted second round funding. These were simply bad ideas or bad companies that were no longer worth speculating on for the sake of building a portfolio.'

Picking up on a couple of specific issues, the report notes that many dotcom companies had limited revenue streams that relied on the internet living up to the hype, not only about the speed of its adoption but the speed at which consumers could access it. Sadly, it didn't live up to the hype.

In addition, Dudley Hawes makes some interesting observations about the funding environment that launched so many seemingly good, yet ultimately disastrous, ideas in the heady days of the internet bubble:

'Venture capitalists and analysts faced considerable difficulty in finding methods of due diligence and project assessment because of the pace and complexity of the deals involved.'

The report also takes a swipe at internet incubators and other get-rich-quick investment vehicles, saying:

'Over time, the perceived wisdom of traditional venture capitalists was undermined by the new entrants' unhealthy tolerance of poor business ideas, weak due diligence and the need for quick wins.'

But Hawes was not all doom and gloom about the dotcom sector and its astonishing collapse. He later told me: 'Some of the ideas weren't all that bad, they just didn't have enough time to prove the concept before the bubble burst. There are some incredibly good propositions out there which really will change the way business is done, and as long as they have the funding and support they will succeed. The real value of all of this is that a lot of offline businesses have now come to understand the value of the internet as another channel to market.'

What the gurus say: Allen Weiss

In an article entitled *Fallacies and Failures: Ways of thinking that doom start-ups* (which can be found on the website MarketingProfs.com), Professor Allen Weiss – an expert in decision-making at the University of Southern California – identifies four ways of thinking that will invariably consign a start-up to the dustbin of history:

- **Anecdotes and intuition:** Saying 'I think this is great, so everyone else will' is not a good way to do market research.
- **Groupthink:** Roughly this is: 'We think the product is great, and anyone who disagrees just doesn't get it. What's more, we'll ignore any evidence that suggests we might be wrong.'
- **Bad analogies:** 'Mobile phones took off, therefore so will electronic books.'
- **Out of the box thinking:** 'The old rules no longer apply.'

THE MAIN CULPRIT?

From all of these studies it's clear that 'bad thinking' is a major factor in the failure of many innovations, product launches and small businesses, and as we'll find out over the next few chapters, there are plenty of ways to get it wrong. But the good news is that bad thinking can be avoided by challenging the assumptions you as an innovator have about yourself, your innovation and the people for whom it is intended.

5

We have the technology, but don't believe the hype

*'Hype and excessive optimism are necessary evils
for driving the technology industry forwards.'*

San Jose Business Journal
11 June 2001

One of the great mantras of the dotcom boom was that traffic on the internet was 'doubling every hundred days'. This 'fact' was trotted out by journalists, analysts and CEOs to illustrate what a profound change was taking place and what a great opportunity it was for investors. After all, who could resist pumping money into an industry that was growing at such a frantic pace? The problem was, it simply wasn't true.

The 'hundred days' myth took off when the statistic was quoted in a document entitled *The Emerging Digital Economy*, which was published by the US Department of Commerce (DoC) in April 1998. With its new found credibility, the myth assumed the status of an indisputable fact and the people who believed it embarked on the biggest and most wasteful investment binge the world has ever seen.

In fact, the DoC document was quoting figures taken from a white paper published by Inktomi Corporation, and they, in turn, were getting their facts from UUNet, an internet infrastructure company owned by WorldCom. As we now know, WorldCom was a company whose executives had a powerful financial incentive to talk up the numbers.

By November 2000, when the 'hundred days' statistic was finally scrutinized by the questioning mind of Andrew Odlyzko (a researcher at AT&T Labs), the damage had been done. Billions had gone up in smoke. Instead of doubling every hundred days, traffic on the internet was actually doubling every year; that's a big difference. Looking back, this myth was probably the most damaging piece of hype in business history, but the irony is that it also underpinned an extraordinarily creative period of innovation in which many new ideas were given a chance to succeed.

THE SEDUCTIVE CHARM OF NEW IDEAS

Hype and innovation walk hand in hand in a relationship that's both necessary and uneasy, as the *San Jose Business Journal* points out in the quote at the beginning of this chapter. Then there's the natural and sometimes excessive optimism that flows from innovation's promise of a brighter world. The bursting of the dotcom bubble shows that hype and excessive optimism are both a blessing and a curse for innovators – they can create a climate of thinking in which innovative ideas are both given a chance and doomed to fail.

The benefits of hyping innovation are numerous – and not just for innovators:

- The innovator's profile is raised, helping the company or organization to raise money.
- This in turn creates new jobs at the company.
- The innovator's backers see an increase in their investment.
- The company may come to market, helping it to raise more money.
- This generates fees for investment banks and, with any luck, investors enjoy an increase in the value of their stake.
- This creates more interest in the market, which in turn encourages other innovators to enter with rival or complementary innovations, creating more jobs.
- The economy becomes more innovative and other 'big ideas' are given a chance.
- Research companies make money by forecasting the growth of new

markets and conference companies stage new events to discuss the implications of the innovation.

- The media gets entertaining stories and the public gets a warm glow thinking how much brighter the future will be thanks to innovation and technology.

However, hyping innovation also has its dangers:

- There will almost inevitably be unrealistic expectations of the innovation's promise and the speed of its diffusion into the market or throughout society as a whole.
- The hype can lead to a frenzied investment environment in which critical analysis is neglected (and even frowned upon).
- This leads to poor quality investment decisions that enable poor quality ideas to survive.
- When innovation fails to live up to the hype, there will be financial losses for investors and job losses for the people involved.
- The disillusionment turns into the inevitable backlash against innovation.
- This in turn creates a more hostile funding climate in which other innovators find it hard to raise money, however good their ideas.
- As a result, the economy becomes less innovative.

This is a typical investment bubble of the sort described in 1841 by Charles Mackay in his classic volume *Extraordinary Popular Delusions and the Madness of Crowds*. The central argument of Mackay's book is that people simply do not learn from the mistakes of the past – an argument that has only been reinforced by the collapse of the dotcom bubble and the rather dubious 'new economy' thinking that led to it. Ignoring the lessons of the past is one of the major reasons why innovation fails today.

THE HYPE CYCLE

The dynamics of hyping innovation are neatly captured in the Hype Cycle, an idea floated in the mid-1990s by the Gartner Group, a research company specializing in growth markets and new technologies.

The Hype Cycle identifies five stages in the early life of innovative technologies:

- A 'technology trigger' like a breakthrough or demonstration of the technology.
- A rapid climb to the 'peak of inflated expectations', fuelled by unrealistic forecasts of its potential, media hype and investor frenzy.
- An equally rapid descent into the 'trough of disillusionment' when people realize that the innovation is not living up to the hype and both investors and the media start the backlash.
- A gradual climb back up the 'slope of enlightenment' as people realize the innovation has some uses after all.
- Finally, the 'plateau of productivity' is reached when the innovation becomes mainstream.

The Gartner Group's Hype Cycle of Emerging Technology

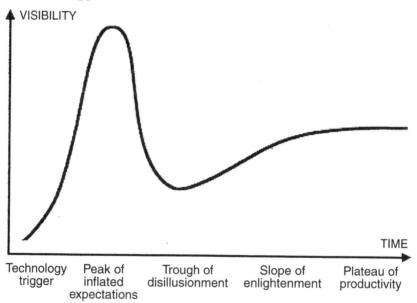

Source: Gartner Group

I'd argue that somewhere in the trough of disillusionment is a 'pit of doom' into which many innovative ideas and business models disappear – just like most dotcoms did.

If the shape of the Hype Cycle looks familiar, think back to the previous chapter and the trends that Neil Rackham identified when he saw innovative new products hitting the market.

In a paper entitled *Why Bad Things Happen to Great New Products*,[1] Rackham argues that success comes because the initial hype has died down:

> 'When sales don't happen, the sales force loses their enthusiasm; all the bells and whistles lose their lustre, the product becomes just another product and attention swings back to the customer. Sales people stop talking and start asking.'

THE HYPE MACHINE

I won't focus on the public relations industry in this section, for a very good reason: PR companies are paid to hype innovation and many of them do it very well, issuing breathless press releases that gush about the wonders of the latest technology.

Instead, the rest of this chapter will focus on the people who should know better than to believe the hype and the people who should be asking the tough questions but frequently don't – the futurists, the analysts and the journalists. All of us (and I include my own career as a journalist) have played a part in hyping innovation when we should have been more sceptical. It's now my belief that we helped to fuel the biggest and most wasteful speculative bubble in history. If the climate has since turned against innovation, we must assume some of the responsibility.

First, however, we need to understand why forecasting is too important to leave to people who seem unable to ask those awkward little questions about how the future will *really* turn out. We have the technology, but should we believe the hype?

THE PERILS OF FORECASTING THE FUTURE

'In accordance with the plan laid down we now proceed to the consideration of the follies into which men have been led by their eager desire to pierce the thick darkness of futurity.'

Charles Mackay
Extraordinary Popular Delusions and the Madness of Crowds

The ability to speculate about the future is what separates humanity from the animal kingdom. By necessity, innovators have to be futurists – they must possess the vision to look ahead and see a future in which their innovation is being used by possibly millions of people. Investors, too, need to look into the future to decide which of today's innovators to back. Governments need to plan and industry needs to have some sense of direction. But the unfortunate fact is that, when it comes to forecasting the future, we really aren't much good. In fact, no less a person than Gideon Gartner, founder of the Gartner Group, once told *Business 2.0* magazine: 'Forecasts are seldom accurate in any field.'[2] Bad forecasts invariably lead to bad planning, bad thinking and bad investments.

The most common error of forecasting the impact of innovation is over-optimism – thinking the world will change more rapidly than it does. It was over-optimism that caused the downfall of many innovative internet companies. Many of the underlying ideas were sound, but they assumed consumers would change long-established habits much more rapidly than they actually did.

In his eloquent critique of the forecasting industry – *Megamistakes: Forecasting and the myth of rapid technological change* – Professor Steven Schnaars estimates that only 20–25% of technological forecasts turn out to be correct. The rest are either wrong or too vague to be evaluated properly (just like astrology!). He observes:

'The successes [of forecasting] tend to be conservative in their outlook, while the failures foresee fantastic changes. The successes call for smaller, slower changes and reject radical innovations.'

Many of these forecasting flops are fun to read. It's the 21st century and we still don't eat dehydrated food or travel in flying cars, and the very computers that were supposed to liberate us from the drudgery of work and the need for paper have generated more of both. And yes, the world market

Plus ça change ... forecasting past and present

In 1969 the US magazine *Industrial Research* asked R&D bosses at leading US corporations to look ten years into the future. For the year 1979, they predicted:

- sustained nuclear fusion to produce power
- manned exploration of Mars and Venus
- extensive use of robots and machines 'slaved' to humans
- room temperature superconductors
- 3D television and holographic movies
- creation of artificial life
- 150–200 year lifespans.

In 2002, futurists at BTexact Technologies made the following predictions, with dates, as part of their annual Technology Timeline:

use of nuclear fusion as a power source	2040
regular manned missions to Mars	2020
robots for housework	2015
room temperature superconductors	2020
3D television/holographic TV	2012/2025
first synthetic (but organic) life form	2003
life expectancy reaches 100	2020

Sources: *Megamistakes*, BTexact

for computers was more than five (contrary to the wisdom of IBM's Thomas J Watson) which shows that some forecasts can be hopelessly conservative – especially those involving computers.

In his book, Schnaars highlights a *Newsweek* special from 1986 that enthused about the intelligent home of the future in which all appliances are networked, food is cooked by remote control and the microwave talks to the bedroom clock. Everything diagnoses itself and calls for the repairman when something goes wrong. But more than 15 years later, almost none of this has happened and yet futurists are still trotting out these same, tired predictions *and being hailed as visionaries for their insights!*

FAILURES OF FICTIONAL FUTURES

Even in fiction, where the imagination can roam free of any real world constraints, we still manage to get our forecasts hopelessly wrong. The year 2001 has been and gone and we still don't have orbiting hotels, bases on the moon and interplanetary spaceships. Videophones – one of futurology's most enduring duff predictions – are still not common and the computers we use are more annoying than Machiavellian.

Ridley Scott's 1982 classic film *Blade Runner* foresees the dark and polluted world of Los Angeles in 2019, complete with flying cars, the slavery of human clones, genetically-designed pets, videophone booths and photo-analyzing computers to which you can say 'enhance'. Yet this dystopian vision of the future is entirely free of mobile phones or any notion of a huge computer network such as today's internet.

THE SPIRIT OF THE AGE

Just as works of science fiction sometimes tell us more about the times in which they were created than the times they foretell, so forecasting is often caught up in the spirit of the age. We all like to think we live in special, revolutionary times; Schnaars describes this as the *zeitgeist* and argues that every era has an exciting new technology that seduces forecasters into making overly optimistic predictions, most of which will turn out to be hopelessly wrong. In the 1950s it was the decade of the jet engine, in the 1960s it was space travel and in the 1970s it was energy. Despite predictions made at the time, we don't drive jet-powered cars, visit hotels in space or plug in to our local neighbourhood nuke for electricity that's too cheap to meter.

Today, the *zeitgeist* is the internet – the idea that the Web is *so* wonderful that everybody and everything will *just have* to be connected to it all the time. Our toasters will download weather maps and burn them into our breakfast; the microwave will call up recipes and ask the fridge to order the ingredients; and soon we'll all be walking around with glasses projecting information into our eyes. Our children will never need to go to school because they can log on to a virtual classroom, and commuting will be a thing of the past, thanks to broadband internet, collaborative groupware and telepresence. The high street will die because we'll all shop online and we'll relax by chatting to our friends in virtual worlds such as Habbo or Entropia.

The technology exists to create this Panglossian future, so naturally it will happen, won't it? Well that's what the visionaries say.

THE PROBLEM WITH TECHNOLOGICAL WONDER!
Steven Schnaars is forthright in his assessment of why technological forecasts are invariably wrong:

> 'The people who made them have been seduced by technological wonder. Most of those forecasts fail because the forecasters fall in love with the technology they are based on and ignore the market the technology is intended to serve. The forecasters who construct them are blinded by their emotions and lose perspective of common sense economic considerations. They are swept away. They incorrectly assume that consumers will find the new technology as enticing and irresistible as they do. In most cases, those assumptions are very wrong.'

In addition, he argues that forecasters continually fail to learn the lessons of the past. Schnaars wrote his book in 1989, long before the internet bubble inflated and then burst so disastrously. A decade later, the visionaries had obviously forgotten the mistakes of the past and, having fallen in love with the technology, once again ignored the foibles of human behaviour and the basic realities of economics, hopelessly overestimating the rate at which everyone else would change.

Another critic of forecasting, Don Norman, points out the naivety of technologists and the assumptions they make about the adoption of future innovations. In his thought-provoking book *Things That Make Us Smart* he says of forecasting:

> 'The easy part of prediction is the technology. The hard part is the social impact.'

While technologists can be forgiven for their lack of insight into human behaviour – they are, after all, technologists, not social scientists – Norman argues that they should at least recognize their shortcomings and bring on board people with a better understanding of human foibles.

Instead of extrapolating where the technology will be in the future, innovators should be asking what social, economic and behavioural forces will actually drive people to use it. Using forecasting techniques such as scenario building is another way to temper technological forecasts with what Steven Schnaars describes as 'a bit of common sense and a well-honed sense of perspective'. Sadly, common sense is often lacking in technological forecasts, especially those intended to grab the headlines.

To give you an example, I've read many forecasts made by futurists in the years I've been observing technology, but one in particular stands out. It was the Barclays Life 20:20 Vision report published in 1998. After a few paragraphs describing how forecasts from the past had proved comically off-target, it then made the following prediction for Britain in the year 2020:

> 'There will be a rail renaissance with 350mph magnetic levitation (Maglev) trains zooming into the major cities.'

At the time it struck me as being such a silly and undisciplined prediction that it could be dismissed with a single word: Railtrack. For those of you who haven't had the misfortune to commute by train in Britain, Railtrack was the privatized owner of the national railway infrastructure. Even back in 1998, when the forecast was made, Railtrack was the most hated company in Britain. In fact, it was such a lame duck that in 2001 it had to be taken over by the government. To think that in 22 years it could turn itself and the network around and run a shiny new Maglev train system was a prediction that didn't stand a minute's critical analysis.

Of course, the forecaster might have considered that someone other than Railtrack might try to make the Maglev miracle happen, but they ignored awkward little details such as the massive investment required (conventional railways lose money and Maglev is *far* more expensive than conventional railways) or the tortured planning process that would be involved. London is a crowded city and the idea of knocking down homes to build new commuter lines and new stations is likely to prove unpopular. Maglev may be a great innovation, but not in my back yard thank you! Still, like all good pop futurology, it made the headlines.

Now, it would be foolhardy to say that the Maglev revolution *won't* happen; far too many people have ended up with egg on their faces dismissing innovations such as powered flight, space travel, the computer and the telephone. As Garage.com founder Guy Kawasaki once said in his *Ten Rules for Revolutionaries*:

'Never say something won't work; it will come back to haunt you.'

Quite right. Perhaps the better strategy is not to say that an innovation will fail, but to question more rigorously why it might succeed. Sometimes, things that seem like great ideas lose their sheen when you start to question the underlying assumptions and ask awkward questions, like 'so what?' or 'who will pay for this?' or 'why would anybody use it?'.

TUNNEL VISIONARIES

The problem with technological forecasting is that it is rarely subjected to such critical analysis. In the business world, futurists are hailed as visionaries and while we need visionaries to push the envelope and at least try to make the future a brighter place for us all, the fact is that being a 'visionary' is a job that comes with a truckload of indulgence. You can predict whatever you like, no matter how naïve or outlandish, and it's highly unlikely anyone will tell you you're talking rubbish – and if they do, your disciples will no doubt accuse them of 'not getting it'. It doesn't matter if you're proved wrong, because you don't have to offer money-back guarantees and by the time your prediction comes due most people will have forgotten what you originally said. Anyway, you can't be proved wrong because you have time and the inevitable march of technology on your side. When the time comes and what you predicted still hasn't happened, all you have to do is sit back and say 'Just wait, it will happen' or 'That's what they said about television/the motor car/powered flight' or any other technology.

> 'We want to believe that tomorrow is going to be better, and although forecasters don't intentionally exploit the fact, it certainly makes their life easier. They have a built-in audience and it's an uncritical audience because it's difficult to tell them they're wrong. If you're generating forecasts and you want journalists to pick them up it's better to make a specific forecast because that's what they want, not just a general prediction that something might happen some time in the future. The point is that you can't be specific and expect to be accurate; timing is usually what's wrong with most forecasts because that's the most difficult variable to take into account.'
>
> David Donnelly
> Lecturer in Media Futures
> University of Houston

Let's face it, if you go to Silicon Valley and shout 'earthquake' often enough you'll eventually be proved right – and then you can tell everyone how clever you were for predicting it. Much futurology is about as insightful.

The other great thing about being a futurist is that you'll always find an audience eager to lap up your predictions, however derivative and hackneyed they are. In his book *What Were They Thinking?* marketing expert Robert McMath warns innovators to 'beware of futurists bearing prognostications', saying:

'There seems to be no end to the conferences and trade shows that need entertainers. The real trick is to be just a tad ahead of your audience. Reinforce the idea they already have, while suggesting you've got an inside track on the information that's driving other marketers' decisions. That's how to ring up the big bucks with private consultations.'

But the fact is we'd all prefer to hear a visionary telling us how we'll all be able to take holidays in space than listen to the nit-picking sceptic who asks awkward little questions like: 'How exactly will you build an orbiting hotel, how much will it cost, what will your cash flows be and who will invest?'

If the technology bubble has proved one thing it's that nobody wants a doomsayer, however rational their arguments and however right they may turn out to be in the end. When the hype reaches fever pitch, the sceptics and realists are invariably drowned out – or even sacked, in the case of one

'Is hype dangerous? Yes, because it's so much easier to think you can throw technology at problems and automate humans out of everything and it will all work out fine. That's ridiculous and naïve and it goes against our everyday experience of technology, which is that the more we have, the more complex things become. Much technology is so poorly conceived and poorly executed that people's lives are not enriched at all. We shouldn't be against technology, just against bad applications and stupid uses for it.'

Paulina Borsook
Author of *Cyberselfish*

Wall Street analyst who suggested that Enron was in trouble several months before it collapsed!

But in such a frenzied environment, an attitude of (supportive) scepticism is exactly what's needed to temper enthusiasm for some of the more hare-brained schemes that people think up. After all, money spent on bad ideas robs good ideas of funding and, as I'll argue in later chapters, those bad ideas can and should be rooted out with a bit of critical thinking.

The problem is this: in the dynamic enterprise culture we have today, it seems that it's always better to try and fail, no matter how badly-researched or misguided your endeavours turn out to be. Indeed, many people – usually the ones who have the luxury of spending someone else's money – argue that's it's essential to fail in order to succeed in later ventures (assuming you actually learned why you failed in the first place!).

But be a pragmatist and ask those awkward little questions and that's the quickest way to find yourself labelled as 'unhelpful', 'boring', 'safe' or 'unenterprising' – a knocker, a doomsayer, a dinosaur, a non-believer or somebody who just doesn't get it. Now you know why people who adopt innovation last of all are the 'laggards', and why the word 'Luddite' is an insult.

You don't think so? Here's a challenge: take a visionary and a doubter. The visionary is a world famous computer scientist who says that by the end of the decade we'll all be walking around with computer screens in our glasses, projecting augmented visual reality on to our eyes so that we can be connected to the internet all the time and receive information about the world around us. It'll beam us money-off coupons from nearby shops whose avatars will float around in augmented reality, telling us what's on offer. What's more, we can use it to check our email, stock prices and the news while we're on the move. The doubter, meanwhile, is a nobody who thinks about it for a second and says: 'Nah, it won't catch on; why does anyone need that kind of stuff?'

Now fast forward to the end of the decade and imagine that the doubter turns out to be right. The glasses we wear are still just glasses – no augmented reality, no virtual world, no 24/7 connection and no avatars beamed on to our retinas. Whose insight was better? The visionary, for having the audacity to imagine such an exciting idea, or the doubter for his pragmatic and ultimately accurate take on how people work in the real world? Now ask yourself which of them you'd rather have listened to in the first place?

If you believed the visionary and built a business around projecting content on to people's eyeballs, and then found there was no market, how would you feel if the doubter turned around and said: 'Well I told you so; everyone else could see it was a stupid idea but you swallowed the hype!' Would your response be: 'Yup, you were right, we misjudged the market completely', or would you become irritated and say: 'Well at least we had the guts to try – what did you do?'

This is why hype and forecasting matter. Believing the hype, getting caught up in the *zeitgeist* and swallowing the wildly optimistic forecasts may allow an explosion of innovative new ideas, and some of them may well be inspired, but for most it's a recipe for disaster. Steven Schnaars hits the nail on the head when he says:

> 'Mistaken forecasts have turned into traps for unsuspecting firms. Instead of opportunities for growth, those mistaken markets have wasted time and money and distracted management from more fruitful endeavours. If innovations and growth markets are the lifeblood of industry, then mistaken forecasts are the viruses that attack that lifeblood.'

Consider the case of WebVan, a company set up to offer online grocery shopping in major American cities. When it came to the market back in late 1999, high up in WebVan's prospectus was a Forrester Research prediction that the US market for online grocery shopping would grow from $235 million in 1998, to $10.8 billion in 2003 – about 2% of the total US grocery market. With figures like that you'd have been crazy not to have wanted a slice of the pie, especially if you felt you could become the nation's favourite online grocer. But the forecast of consumer uptake proved hopelessly optimistic and having invested so heavily up front – on distribution centres and brand building – WebVan faced a huge mismatch between its expenditure and its revenues.

This optimism proved fatal and WebVan went bankrupt in the summer of 2001, having spent more than a billion dollars of someone else's money. Of course, if the forecast had been more conservative – in November 2001, Forrester revised the figure to $5.8 billion – would WebVan have been able to raise so much money when it floated? And if two competing market forecasts had been available to them – $10.8 billion and the more conservative $5.8 billion – which do you think they would have put in their prospectus?

INDEPENDENT ANALYSTS?

It's important to remember that market forecasters have their own agendas. The frenzied rush to float internet companies exposed the shameful truth that many Wall Street research analysts were more than willing to suspend disbelief entirely and cash in the integrity of their work for a share of the fat flotation bonuses that came with every Initial Public Offering. Of course they were going to put a gloss on business models that were little short of absurd – they were shouting 'Buy Buy Buy' because in those heady days, the honest and critical analysis of internet stocks was bad for business, bad for their bonuses and probably bad for their career prospects. Wall Street made a packet selling shoddy goods at inflated prices to undiscerning investors, who were more than willing to swallow the hype. As long as shares kept going up, who cared? Everyone was making money and nobody wanted a party-pooper! Even 'independent' market forecasting companies have their own agendas – selling reports and consultancy services. If several companies come out with increasingly optimistic forecasts for a particular market, it's easy to get swept up in the trend for higher and higher figures. That's what grabs the headlines and sells reports.

To be fair to market forecasters, coming up with hard figures is difficult and many clients buying their research may actually consider the accuracy of their forecasts to be less important than the trends that they identify. Just as the American pioneers headed 'west' – they weren't aiming for Main Street, Santa Monica – so innovators and start-ups need a general sense of direction, not a detailed road map with a particular destination in mind. The problems arise when that general sense of direction turns out to be completely wrong, as was the case with forecasts of the growth of smart cards or the idea that oil would run out early in the 21st century.

Predicting the future isn't easy, even when you're using the best techniques. Futurists and research companies don't pluck forecasts out of thin air. Don't forget that technologies can take unforeseen turns and find unexpected new markets, which makes the life of the forecaster even more difficult. When lasers were first invented, who would have thought they would one day be used for playing films? Then there are technological wild cards: Thomas J Watson's prediction for a world market of just five computers was eminently reasonable in an era when computers ran on valves and were the size of houses. It wasn't that he lacked any insight – far from it; the invention of transistors and then microchips made a mockery of his forecast, as did the computer's migration from the laboratory to the home, from calculating machine to entertainment centre.

Forecasting methods: How the seers predict the future
Futurists use several different methods to forecast technological progress, with varying degrees of failure:

- **Extrapolation:** At its simplest, extrapolation says: 'The technology is here now and it will be there in the future', which is fine for predicting the speed of computer processors (using Moore's Law) but which is vulnerable to fads, fashions and technological wild cards. Simple technological extrapolation fails to take human behaviour into account.
- **Delphi:** A technique that solicits the opinions of experts in relevant fields, usually through questionnaires and follow-up discussions. The results of the questionnaires are summarized and sent back to the experts who can re-evaluate their contributions after seeing what other experts have written. It assumes that experts are good at forecasting the future of their own fields.

- **Analogies:** Using knowledge about the spread of one technology to forecast the spread of another. This technique must be used with care, as bad analogies can lead to disastrous forecasts. For example, does the rapid growth of the wired internet hold any clues for the growth of the wireless internet?
- **Scenario building:** This is one of the more successful techniques, in which a number of possible futures are brainstormed, with perhaps two to four being presented as alternatives. This allows those using the forecast to evaluate for themselves all the different possibilities and the assumptions behind them. Although many scenarios are presented with probabilities, there is an argument that this can lead to a false sense of certainty about the future.
- **Probabilities:** Some forecasts are expressed in the following terms: 'There is a 70% probability that Technology X will be adopted by 50% of the market by 2010'.

Gartner Group analyst Alex Linden says the real value of forecasts is to help companies prepare for the future, however accurate their predictions turn out to be. He says: 'If I make a prediction and it helps you to prepare the right way, then that forecast has had a positive effect, even if the numbers don't turn out the way I thought.'

Another forecaster, Ian Pearson of BT, says that much popular futurology is there to give us a sense of what *might* be, not what *will* be – and the gulf between the two is down to human behaviour and economics. He admits that his public and corporate roles are different. As a pop futurist his job is to grab headlines and provoke discussion about the future; his website is full of essays about how people will navigate supermarkets using GPS (Global Positioning System) and shop with virtual reality headsets. But in his corporate role as a strategic forecaster, Pearson says it's necessary to separate the headline grabbing hype from the reality of how people will accept technologies in the future. 'There's frivolous futurology, which is there for entertainment, and there's a more serious side which is all about understanding how our company can survive,' he explains of his role in BT. 'What we do is try to create products that will make the world a better place – in our opinion, of course. Some people may consider it a technological nightmare but it's our right as a company to try to push things in the direction we think is right. If people don't like that, they are free to try to create an alternative future.'

Betting on the future

In April 2002, a Californian organization called the Long Bets Foundation challenged futurists to put their money where their mouth is and back their predictions with hard cash on the Longbets.org website. The Foundation's aims are laudable: to encourage more responsible and accountable forecasting and stimulate debate about the future. The site offers sceptics a chance to challenge grandiose forecasts made by 'visionaries' and hopes to develop a better understanding of the nature of forecasting.

THE TROUBLE WITH 'GEE WHIZZ' JOURNALISM

If forecasts suffer from over-optimism, it should be down to the media to restore some sanity to the world. Too often, however, I believe we have been far too credulous. In the popular press, the reporting of innovation and technology is less about critical analysis and more about the 'gee whizz' factor; it's about entertaining readers with the promise of a brighter future thanks to the marvels of technology and science. Most folk who write about technology are gadget-toting enthusiasts who suffer from pro-innovation bias. It makes us feel cool to have the latest toys and hang out with the people we believe are shaping the future of the world. It makes us feel special to be on the cutting edge. It's not surprising, therefore, that we inevitably present technology as a force for good, with little discussion of its failures or its unintended consequences. Nor is it surprising that we believe that everyone else will share our views and see technology through our own, rose-tinted spectacles – of course everyone will want to buy that cool wireless gadget so they can be connected to the internet every minute of the day.

In the mainstream media, the journalism of innovation is the journalism of how things work and what implications there might be for the future. We focus on invention and innovation, not diffusion into the market. We're happy to quote the market forecasts because they're the best figures we have and we assume that a certain amount of diligence has gone into their preparation.

But sometimes, we can't help getting caught up in the hype because it's so entertaining. We like to let our imaginations run riot, write articles that extrapolate the technology's possibilities and speculate about every possible use for which it might be deployed. And these kinds of articles are invariably written with no regard for the realities of human behaviour or basic economics, because that would spoil the fun, wouldn't it?

To give you an example, think of Nanotechnology. You've probably read articles that trotted out the brighter future it will bring, when tiny little nanosubmarines like the one on *Fantastic Voyage* sail through your blood-stream digging away at plaque on your arteries so you'll live a longer and more productive life. But in any of those articles, did you ever read how those little excavators would stop digging when they came to the artery wall itself? Did you ever read about how the immune system might react to the presence of tiny submarines in the bloodstream, or whether people might actually object to being infused with nanoprobes for fear of something going horribly and fatally wrong? Probably not.

Then there's the orbiting hotel. Every so often someone recycles the story about a plan to build a hotel in space using empty fuel tanks from the space shuttle. I've yet to read how the darn thing will actually be built, because one thing's for certain, if you want to build a hotel in space, you need to build a space station first to house the workers. That's a significant and expensive project in itself, as NASA is finding out. Then there are those inconvenient little details, such as the fact that fuel tanks from the shuttle are designed to fall back to earth and getting them to stay up there in orbit would involve a lot of extra cost that NASA or other investors might not be willing to bear. Still, why should a few awkward questions get in the way of an otherwise entertaining story – and anyway, technology will take care of all those problems because technology always gets better.

But a more interesting issue is this: should we be writing unhelpful, knocking copy about well-intentioned and enterprising people who are trying their best to make the world a better place – however misguided their assumptions and however unsuccessful their ideas may eventually turn out to be? Surely we should be encouraging the risk-takers, the innovators and the visionary thinkers, not attacking them!

PUNCTURING THE HYPE

Hype and optimistic forecasts are a double-edged sword. They can create a climate of great innovation and challenging new ideas, but beware of the inevitable backlash. Even with no-brain innovations, change can take longer than you think – whether it's the cure for scurvy or dropping the Saturday morning shopping run to buy the groceries online. But here are a few tips to help you avoid being caught up in the hype:

- Don't be seduced by technology – just because it exists, it doesn't mean people will buy it or use it. Technological forecasts rarely take human foibles into account.
- Remember that much technology journalism is there for entertainment and naturally tends to overstate the impact of any new technology with wide-eyed projections. What real people do in the real world is another matter.
- Keep a sense of perspective. Step back and ask: 'Does this really make sense?'
- The simplest questions are always the toughest, like: 'Who will use this, and why?'
- Think of the cost-benefit equation. Great technology does not guarantee great profits.
- Visionary thinking is vital for a healthy and innovative economy, but it's no vaccine against making stupid predictions or silly mistakes. Even visionaries get it horribly wrong sometimes.

- Don't ignore proven statistics: growth forecasts are usually wrong, most new products fail and, unfortunately, doomsayers are usually right (unless they're environmentalists, whose gloomy forecasts rarely turn out as bad as they predict).
- Consider the forecaster's agenda; is it to grab headlines, generate investment banking fees, sell reports or create markets?
- The following phrases should ring alarm bells:

  i. 'We'll all be...' (using some kind of technology or service in the future)
  ii. 'New Era' or 'New Economy'
  iii. 'It's different this time'.

- When you read about innovation in the media, draw up a list of five tough questions the journalist didn't ask.

The hyping of 'It'

No chapter on hyping innovation would be complete without mentioning the Segway Human Transporter – possibly the most hyped piece of technology in history. Unveiled in December 2001, the Segway can most simply be described as an electric scooter with parallel wheels and a lot of very clever electronics and gyroscopic technology to keep its rider from falling over.

The hype began earlier that year when rumours on the internet suggested that its inventor, Dean Kamen, had been offered $250,000 just to co-write a book on the machine – code named 'It' or 'Ginger' – which had supposedly taken ten years to develop. Although Kamen remained tight-lipped about his invention, his reputation as a truly brilliant inventor only helped to fuel speculation, which really took off when bulletin boards such as TheITQuestion were inundated with outlandish theories that it was a personal hovercraft, an anti-gravity device or even a personal jet pack.

The hyperbole was heightened by comments made by those 'in the know', including Apple founder Steve Jobs, Amazon founder Jeff Bezos and the noted venture capitalist John Doerr. Apparently, the mysterious machine would be 'bigger than the internet', it would require cities to be re-built around it, and it would make Kamen richer than Microsoft's Bill Gates in the space of just five years. With such plaudits (could even a perpetual motion engine live up to hype like that?) it was not surprising that when the machine was finally unveiled it was met with a mixture of acclaim and derision in the press. 'Is that it?' was a common cry, along with the suggestion that anyone riding it would be paying $5,000 to look like a complete dork. Within months it had been featured in an episode of *Frasier* and been mercilessly lampooned in the scurrilous cartoon series *South Park*.

In fact, what came to be known as the Segway Human Transporter is a brilliantly innovative piece of technology. Stand on it and lean forwards and it moves; lean back and it stops, twist and it turns, reading your every move. Weighing around 85lb, the Segway can travel more than 15 miles on its batteries and get up to 12.5mph on the footpath. Kamen believes his invention will reduce the need for cars over short distances.

Kamen hopes that the first customers will be the US Postal Service, police forces and maybe theme parks – assuming, of course, that they think it has a better cost-benefit proposition than rival (and cheaper) technologies such as bicycles, micro-scooters, motor scooters and Go-Peds.

What was particularly interesting about the Segway was the response it provoked on the bulletin boards. Flame wars erupted between those who believed the hype and those who thought it was a loser. Some of the insults were fascinating, particularly one that sneered: 'You obviously work for someone else, I can't imagine what that must be like!' Another supporter, responding to the suggestion that Kamen might not have done any market research, wrote: 'You're obviously the kind of person who actually cares what other people think', to which came the reply: 'Yes, I'm a venture capitalist; we call it due diligence.'

What these and many other messages illustrated was the belief that whether the Segway was the greatest invention ever, or a complete joke, criticizing an innovator of Kamen's stature was a crime akin to burning the American flag or telling mom her apple pie tastes crap!

As to the future of the Segway, it remains to be seen whether it becomes the Model T or the Tucker of human transportation. It has recently been awarded the 2002 'Best of What's New' award by *Popular Science* magazine and taken part in a high profile Amazon.com promotion. Even if the Segway fails, the innovative technology that keeps it upright could prove to be the solution to an entirely different problem.

But as for cities being re-engineered and Kamen becoming richer than Bill Gates, step back and ask yourself a simple question: do you really think that's likely?

NOTES

1   Available at www.huthwaite.com.
2   *Business 2.0* magazine, July 2001.

6

How bad thinking kills good ideas

'Give a whopping bonus to the person who tells you something you really don't want to hear. It may be the most prudent investment you'll ever make.'

Robert McMath
What Were They Thinking?

Excessive optimism and believing the hype are two forms of bad thinking that curse innovations long before they reach the market. But between the idea and the user there are many other ways in which bad thinking can trip up the unwary innovator. As we've noted before, the fact that so many innovations fail begs the question whether they should have come to market in the first place.

In this chapter we'll think about why innovators make the often disastrous assumptions they do, why many of them don't learn from the mistakes of the past, why they become trapped in losing strategies and why they ignore evidence that's yelling at them to give up. In doing so we'll look at factors such as overconfidence, ego involvement, escalation bias and groupthink; but first, let's consider bad ideas.

SOME IDEAS REALLY DO SUCK!

Throughout this book I've been trying not to rubbish anyone's ideas or suggest that innovators are stupid for coming up with concepts that the rest of us might dismiss with a moment's thought. Apart from suffering a pro-innovation bias and a firm belief in the supremacy of entrepreneurial capitalism, I've already argued that success and failure are very much functions of time, space and perception. What may seem crazy now can become mainstream for another generation, and while there's currently a backlash against the kinds of ideas that were floated in the dotcom bubble, there's no doubt many of them will have their day ... eventually.

But the inescapable fact is, some ideas really *are* stupid. Instead of being patented or brought to market they should have been stuffed in a rock-filled sack and thrown off the nearest bridge. Take the male contraceptive plug, for example. United States Patent 5,701,914 describes a tiny device that works in a similar fashion to those stoppers you push into wine bottles to make sure the plonk doesn't go flat. Push it in, flick a lever and it expands to form a seal. Incredibly, someone (a man at that!) spent time and money thinking it up, drafting the diagrams and filing the patent because he honestly believed that other men would use it! Why???

If the male contraceptive plug sounds absurd, is it any more stupid than spending $100 to sell goods worth $50 or giving free computers to people and asking them to look at advertising in return? A company called FreePC tried that in the dotcom boom and quickly went bust. But if that sounds stupid, what about iPhysician.net, which gives PCs to doctors in return for them receiving marketing information about drugs?

Is the plug any more stupid than the idea of implanting a wireless chip into your brain so you can download your email and surf the net? There are respectable – nay 'visionary' – computer scientists who think this is the way forward.

Yet trawl through the Patent Office (or better still, the TotallyAbsurd.com website) and you'll find a host of equally silly ideas: there's US Patent 4,176,537 – a golf club with a shotgun cartridge in the head for that extra oomph off the tee. Then there's US Patent 4,605,000, which looks like a spaceman's helmet but with the addition of plants inside to generate oxygen. And what about US Patent 4,465,089 – a motorized wheel to propel roller skaters, which the inventor describes as 'A driving vehicle by which the skater may enjoy skating by being pulled or pushed'.

Why did anyone bother investing time and money to patent such obviously daft inventions? Didn't they ask themselves simple questions like who will use this and why? How did they come to believe there might be any kind of market for products as bizarre as these? Assuming there aren't hordes of comedy inventors devising nonsensical contraptions just to give us all a laugh, what can we learn from the male contraceptive plug and ideas like it?

Andy Gibbs, whose PatentCafe website is a useful online resource for inventors, thinks many of the sillier ideas come from amateur inventors for whom getting a patent is reward enough for their endeavours. They have an idea, run it by their friends – who naturally tell them it's great – and then embark on the patenting and prototyping process. 'Whether it will fly or whether they make any money is incidental,' says Gibbs. 'What matters is that they have had an idea and getting a patent is a form of validation for them. They grab that little bit of success and hold on to it, and that insulates them from the possibility it might fail if it ever reached the market.'

THE PERILS OF PUSHING THE ENVELOPE

To be an innovator is to be endowed with characteristics the rest of the population either doesn't have or doesn't use. Truly successful innovators have to think ahead, spot opportunities, take big risks and *persist*, often in the face of doubts and conventional wisdom. The trouble is that these characteristics can bring problems of their own.

Until now I've used the term 'innovator' to mean both inventors and entrepreneurs, but for a moment I'll drop the rather artificial taxonomy to make a couple of points. Think of a typical inventor; what comes to mind? Someone like Doc, the eccentric boffin from *Back to the Future*? Or maybe you have in mind someone rather nerdy who beavers away all day in R&D? Does either description strike you as portraying someone in touch with the needs and wants of the rest of the population? Probably not.

Luckily, most inventors don't fit the stereotype. Many of them got into the game because they were trying to solve problems that they were grappling with themselves. What they had was *empathy* and *insight*, which they combined with technical know-how to solve the problem. One of the best examples is Sam Farber, who developed the OXO Good Grips line of kitchen tools after seeing his wife Betsey having difficulty with conventional tools because of her arthritis. Realizing that 40 million other Americans had the same problem, Farber created a set of tools whose handles were easier and more comfortable for older and arthritic people to grip.

I've met plenty of innovative technologists and I can't think of one I'd describe as a socially dysfunctional dweeb. On the other hand, I wouldn't describe them as being 'typical users' either – or indeed, typical people. Remember there are five categories of adopters, ranging from 'innovators' to 'laggards'. If anything, the technologists are a more extreme form of the innovators that Everett Rogers characterized as venturesome, daring, risky, technologically proficient, able to cope with uncertainty and able to absorb financial losses from innovations that fail.

Now the point is this: if you're a dynamic young entrepreneur developing technology's 'next big thing', with which of these five groups of users do you feel the most affinity? Do you feel any empathy with the conservative 'late majority' and the positively Luddite 'laggards' who together make up 50% of the market? Do you think they will share your appetite for news-on-the-go or for constant connectivity to the internet and email? Are they as happy with high technology as you are?

Bear in mind that most internet companies didn't fail because they had *no* customers, they failed because they didn't have *enough* before the money ran out. If you can build a business serving only the most hardcore early adopters, then fine. If you can't, read on.

Anthropologist Lucy Suchman spent two decades observing innovators in action at Xerox's legendary technological hothouse, the Palo Alto Research Center, which is credited with the invention of graphical interfaces and the computer mouse. Now a Professor of Anthropology at the University of Lancaster, she says that many innovators are so enamoured with technology that they lose sight of what is really important – what people want from technology, not what it can actually do. 'Innovators are very self-referential,' she says, drawing on her experience of seeing them at close quarters. 'They talk to each other and look to each other for an assessment of the value and newness of what they are doing, so it's a very closed system. This means that they end up with a limited and simplistic understanding of their prospective users.'

THE DANGERS OF SELF PROJECTION

Nowadays, larger companies such as Intel, Microsoft and Motorola employ anthropologists to find out how people use technology *in the real world* because focus groups are not always a reliable indicator of how people actually behave, what they really buy etc. Smaller companies, entrepreneurs and inventors don't have that luxury and so there's a very real danger of self-projection – thinking: 'I would use this, so everyone else will'. The technical term for this is 'need bias' and it's the difference between what the customer actually wants and what the innovator *thinks* they want. Need bias was probably at the root of many consumer e-commerce failures. It's probably not an over-simplification to suggest that many cash-rich, time-poor dotcommers were thinking: 'I'm too busy to go out shopping – I'd rather do it all online,' and they assumed that everyone else would too.

Another danger of self-projection is to assume that everyone has the same technical ability and the same feeling of ease around technology as you have. People may hate fighting through the crowds at the supermarket, but if they hate computers even more they're unlikely to flock to websites like Tesco.com, however convenient home shopping may be.

In *The Invisible Computer* – an impassioned plea for human-centred product design – Don Norman points out that as technologies evolve they should become easier to use. This is a reflection of the technical proficiency and the needs of the five categories of adopter. The 'innovators' are happy to download buggy beta software but the 'late majority' want something more reliable and a lot simpler. Unfortunately, many technologists equate product evolution with 'cool new features', but in the real world most of us don't use even half of the features that exist. Just think about a software package like Microsoft Office, or all those strange sub-menus on your mobile. Even the humble washing machine has far more features than most of us will ever need. Yet when the next versions come along, do you think they'll have more cool features or will the manufacturers finally wake up and offer us a cut-down product at a cut-down price?

Technologists try to reassure us that technology will always become better and more user-friendly, but here's the point: if the user manual gets 10% fatter with every upgrade it doesn't appear to be getting any easier, does it? And as we've seen before, Neil Rackham's research on sales pitches indicates that selling a product on new features alone is a losing strategy.

Of course, the best way to find out what customers really want is to ask them, but as we've already discovered, many innovators choose not to. In the absence of decent market research, what you're left with is your perception of what people want; but your perception can be clouded in many different ways.

THE OVERCONFIDENT ENTREPRENEUR

Entrepreneurs are overconfident – they have to be. With so many hurdles to cross and so many doubters to prove wrong, it's in their very nature to take risks, to be headstrong, have masses of self-belief, a restless drive, boundless optimism and a can-do attitude. No one gets rich having poor self-esteem and a pessimistic outlook.

Overconfidence exists in many walks of life. Ask people about their driving abilities and they'll doubtless rate themselves 'above average'. Statistically, this is nonsense, because for an average to exist some people must be below it – but who would admit to being a bad driver? Studies have shown beyond doubt that entrepreneurs are more overconfident than managers. Ask them a question with two possible answers and both groups will give the correct answer with about the same frequency. But ask them how confident they are about their answer and you'll soon see the difference – entrepreneurs will score significantly higher than managers. (Rationally, you should be 50% confident if you don't know the answer for sure, but entrepreneurs aren't rational, thank heavens!).

Natural and essential though it is, however, overconfidence can be the downfall of many great ideas because it embraces a range of potentially disastrous thinking strategies that can condemn even the most innovative concepts to the scrap heap. So, you're an entrepreneur, beware of the following traps:

- ego involvement with the project
- over-optimism about the product and the market's demand for it
- ignoring what the market and the environment are telling you
- groupthink and ignoring feedback from others
- holding on to losers.

In earlier chapters I highlighted the fact that poor market research is one of the biggest factors in the failure of innovations. It was a problem in the 1970s and, despite improvements in market research techniques since then, it still is. What's more, the failure rate for new products has remained at around 85% in spite of improved marketing techniques, better management education, vastly improved product development processes and new ways to understand consumer behaviour; so what's going on? According to one researcher, it's 'ego'.

EGO AND THE FAILURE OF INNOVATION

Much of the research into the success and failure of new products has focused on the management and execution of the product development process. The failure to perform adequate market and consumer research is usually regarded as an issue of management competence. But a marketing expert at the University of Iowa suggests that there is another explanation. According to Professor Randall Schultz, product managers become so ego-involved that they treat the product development process as a pet project and this inevitably clouds their judgement.

'There's a lot of hype associated with new products, but the fact is the failure rate in the US for frequently purchased branded goods remains at about 85%,' he explains. 'This means that the products obviously weren't as good as their champions were saying. Even though the market research techniques are getting better, my argument is that when humans look at the data through the lens of ego involvement, they always overestimate, no matter what the figures say.'

In a number of academic papers on ego involvement, viewpoint and reality, Schultz offers some common-sense observations on the ways that bad thinking can kill innovation. 'To be an entrepreneur you need a lot of self-confidence to feel that you're right,' he explains, adding that many entrepreneurs can also be arrogant, egotistical and insular. 'The more ego-involved you are, the more confident you will be, the more in control you will feel and this means you will take more risks.'

By definition, he says, all innovators are ego-involved in their projects – just as academics are ego-involved in their theories and writers are ego-involved in their books. It's natural for people to experience personal feelings towards projects in which they're investing lots of time and energy. Of course, we want them to succeed because it enhances our feelings of importance and self-esteem and if the project fails we will feel hurt.

The problem, says Schultz, is that ego involvement inevitably seduces innovators into an overly optimistic view of the project and its chances of success. Even if they undertake market research they will tend to look on the bright side, whatever the consumers say. 'I teach a class of students who can spot bad ideas right away,' says Schultz. 'So why can't marketing vice-presidents who get paid $500,000 a year? It's not that the students are any smarter, it's because they are less biased and less ego-involved.'

Schultz has developed a useful concept – 'viewpoint' – which he uses to illustrate the fact that there are three ways to look at the same set of data:

- **Optimistic:** Things are brighter than the numbers suggest.
- **Realistic:** Things are exactly as the numbers suggest.
- **Pessimistic:** Things are worse than the numbers suggest.

Be warned, however, that before viewpoint kicks in, the ego-involved innovator may have selectively chosen the most flattering set of numbers to work with. There may be other less heartening sets of data and these will be selectively ignored. Thus, it's possible to take an overly optimistic view of an overly optimistic set of figures.

The following rather simple matrix shows how this can work.

Ego involvement	Data	Perceived score	Viewpoint
		80	Optimistic
High	70	*70*	Realistic
		60	Pessimistic
		70	Optimistic
Medium	60	*60*	Realistic
		50	Pessimistic
		60	Optimistic
Neutral	50	*50*	Realistic
		40	Pessimistic
		50	Optimistic
Low	40	*40*	Realistic
		30	Pessimistic
		40	Optimistic
Opposed	30	*30*	Realistic
		20	Pessimistic

The figures in the second column represent data from five different market studies of consumer enthusiasm for the product. The mean consumer approval score is 50, but the highly ego-involved entrepreneur selectively chooses the most flattering data, showing a score of 70. From this point there are three different ways to view the data, giving *perceived* scores of 80, 70 and 60, depending on the level of optimism.

There are, of course, perfectly good reasons for taking such a rosy view of the project: it's a useful strategy for motivating the troops and ensuring you have sufficient resources. Schultz also points out that ego involvement can actually increase the chances of success if managers devote more marketing effort to the project than it actually deserves. There's nothing wrong with that as long as you understand the pitfalls and develop strategies to counteract the threats that ego involvement and over-optimism can pose.

BEWARE OF GROUPTHINK

Related to overconfidence and ego involvement is a phenomenon called 'groupthink' which, you'll recall, decision-making expert Allen Weiss cited as a sure-fire killer of start-ups. The notion of groupthink was floated by social psychologist Irving Janis in the early 1970s. At the time he was fascinated by the fact that groups of obviously smart people could arrive at obviously dumb decisions, even though there was compelling evidence to suggest they were about to make a serious mistake. Janis focused on political decision-making, such as the Bay of Pigs fiasco and the refusal to recognize signs of an imminent attack on Pearl Harbor. But the fact is that groupthink exists everywhere that groups of people make decisions under pressure.

The kind of group that is most susceptible to groupthink is a cohesive bunch of people, with similar ideals and working under pressure towards a common goal – just like a typical start-up, in fact! The group's common ambition can lead members to switch off critical thinking, discount any evidence that they might be wrong and ignore alternative ways of thinking. In this way, the group builds a consensus and increases its cohesion. Like hype and overconfidence, it's a double-edged sword that needs to be understood. Acknowledging that groupthink exists and recognizing its symptoms is vital if innovators are to avoid its potentially disastrous effects.

Janis identified eight symptoms of groupthink that can affect any group of people, not just entrepreneurs:

- **The illusion of invulnerability:** We're going to change the world.
- **Belief in the inherent morality of the group:** We know we're right.
- **Finding ways to rationalize bad decisions:** We need new thinking – this is the 'New Economy'.
- **Stereotyping of outsiders:** Those dinosaurs just don't get it.
- **Self-censorship of opinions:** Because you want to be a 'team player'.
- **The illusion of unanimity:** Because team players play the game.
- **Intolerance of dissenters:** Because no one wants a doomsayer!
- **Mind guards to protect the group from inconvenient facts or negative opinions:** You'll find them on every investor bulletin board, flaming people who criticize the company.

It's a useful list to keep handy – especially if you're working in a start-up. Try taking it into your next meeting and award yourself ten points for each symptom you identify. If you score 60 or above it might be a good idea to brush up your résumé!

Looking a little more closely, the first two symptoms exhibit over-confidence in the group and over-estimation of its abilities; the third and fourth are signs of a closed mind and the remainder are pressures towards conformity. Although Janis believed all eight symptoms should be present before diagnosing groupthink, any one of them can be dangerous on its own, let alone in combination with others.

A major malfunction

One of the most tragic examples of groupthink in action was the decision to launch the Space Shuttle Challenger in January 1986. The rocket scientists who actually built the Challenger's solid rocket boosters advised against launching the Shuttle in the unusually cold weather that swept over Florida that week. They warned NASA engineers that crucial seals called O-rings could not be guaranteed to work properly once they had been subjected to freezing temperatures. NASA's engineers already felt under pressure to launch what was a very high-profile mission – a civilian teacher was on board and millions of American schoolchildren would tune in to see her blast off. A previous launch attempt had been scrubbed and there was an air of anticipation around the Cape. NASA's engineers pressured their counterparts at Thiokol, the manufacturer, who went off into a huddle and eventually came back with the 'correct' decision – to launch the Shuttle. Almost immediately after launch the seals began to fail and 73 seconds into the flight the mission came to a disastrous end when one O-ring disintegrated, allowing hot gases to burn through the Shuttle's liquid fuel tank. The ensuing explosion destroyed the spacecraft and seven heroic astronauts were killed – all because of bad thinking that could have been avoided.

Innovators in start-ups are particularly vulnerable to groupthink, according to Professor Nick Chater, director of the Institute for Applied Cognitive Sciences at Warwick University in England. 'The worst form of groupthink is where you have a group that's closed to outsiders, and this is typical of start-ups where all the members of the group are technically specialized and working under conditions of some confidentiality,' he explains.

Another potential problem is the inspiring and visionary leader: precisely those qualities that make them great entrepreneurs can prove disastrous when it comes to making important decisions. 'It's particularly disastrous if the leader doesn't tolerate dissent or being questioned,' says Chater. In fact, dissent can sometimes be regarded as treachery in pull-together start-ups, especially if the traitor is an employee rather than a founder. 'Any group that pins its colours to the same mast is likely to have the attitude that "you're either for us, or against us",' warns Chater. 'It's very hard for them to accept any kind of feedback or any notion that they might be wrong.'

'Being in a start-up is a pretty intense experience and why they typically fail is because they don't keep sticking their heads out of the maelstrom to take a look at the rest of the world. One person starts a company with what they think is a good idea and they find another half dozen people who also think it's a good idea, but unless they're considering the million other people who also have to think it's a good idea they are going to fail. Just a few people saying "This is great" isn't enough.'

Colin Burns
Head of Office, Ideo London

In fact, not listening to feedback is a root cause of many start-up failures, according to Professor Terri Kurtzberg, who studies organizational management at Rutgers University in New Jersey. She believes that group members can be too much alike and argues that the innovation process can be enhanced by having a more diverse team in which conflicts are properly managed. The technical director might squabble with the head of marketing, but at least they know the game, and having some internal tension can help the decision-making process. 'Teams that are more homogenous are the ones in which everyone likes each other, they all see eye to eye and they think that they're being really creative,' she says. 'But if you use objective measures it's the teams that aren't getting along together that actually do better.'

The problem with feedback is that it is often difficult to take, because it feels like a personal attack. She suggests that innovators make feedback part of the innovation process so that everyone will accept it as a matter of course.

Timing and office politics are issues to consider. If feedback is too early it can stifle the creative process, which is why brainstorming sessions should always include the rule 'no criticism, anything goes'. Too late and the feedback can be irrelevant and distracting. Office hierarchies can present problems too: who should offer feedback – a colleague or a superior, and from the same department or a different part of the company?

If taking feedback can be hard, giving it can be even harder, argues Kurtzberg. 'The problem is that the people who are giving the feedback often forget that it is difficult for the other person to take. They have the attitude "I'm doing this for your own good" and that's just wrong; it activates a defence mechanism in the other person.' One good idea, she says, is to offer the feedback in writing; in face-to-face meetings the person receiving the feedback can become too defensive.

COGNITIVE DISSONANCE

The bad thinking strategies outlined in this chapter will eventually lead the unwary innovator to a condition that psychologists call 'cognitive dissonance' – the conflict between what the evidence actually says and what the innovator believes to be the reality. Roughly, this is the feeling you get when market research or, even worse, early sales figures tell you that there's no demand for your product; and because you're an overconfident, overly optimistic and ego-involved entrepreneur, it's a very unpleasant feeling!

Let's face it, you put in all those hours of blood, sweat and tears, you did the killer presentation so many times you started dreaming it, you raised the seed finance, set up an office, hired the best staff you could, developed a fantastic prototype and now you find that nobody wants to buy it.

So what can you do about it? How do you make the unpleasant feeling go away? Well, you have two choices:

- **You can give up and walk away,** which forces you to accept the possibility that you were wrong all along, and that you've just wasted a large part of your life, as well as a serious amount of your money (or if you were lucky, someone else's money). Your dreams of wealth and freedom are in tatters and the future looks especially bleak because the management consultancy you used to work for has a recruitment freeze on and you're unlikely to get your old job back. You've been defeated even before you got to launch the product.
- **You can ignore the evidence** because it's a great product really, the punters just don't get it, but they will when you launch it. Anyway, market research doesn't tell you anything worthwhile does it, and you can't give up now because you've invested so much.

It's a no-brainer, isn't it?

Nick Chater explains: 'There's a natural tendency for people to want to reduce the dissonance, but one of the dangers is that you avoid any evidence that conflicts with what you believe, or you might even avoid the possibility of finding that evidence.'

'The longer it goes on, the worse it will become because you have already put so much work in, and so the tension between the effort you've invested and the problems you might discover gets all the more painful.' So putting off market research is only going to lead to greater problems, not least because when you finally get the results you'll kick yourself for not acting sooner when you knew you should have.

Sue Robson of the UK's Market Research Society admits that doing proper research is a potentially frightening experience for innovators. 'There's a certain kind of entrepreneurial spirit that wants to go ahead and do things regardless of what people say,' she notes. For the few exceptional entre-preneurs whose gut feeling and market knowledge proves exactly right, this self-belief is justified; but for the vast majority it is not. 'That's one of the dangers of doing market research,' says Robson. 'It can tell you something you don't want to hear.'

Now do you understand why so many innovators don't do proper market research? Remember that it should encompass a competitor and price survey, an estimate of market size and a study of the customer's needs and wants. Bigger companies with well-established processes for innovation and new product development will do market research as a matter of course, although some can afford simply to launch products into the market and hope that they stick. Small business entrepreneurs and inventors don't have that luxury.

KNOWING WHEN TO HOLD, WHEN TO FOLD AND WHEN TO WALK AWAY

The 'ignore the evidence' option outlined earlier may sound like a caricature, but the history of innovation is full of product launches that really shouldn't have happened. One of the classic examples is the Premier smokeless cigarette launched by RJ Reynolds in the late 1980s. The alarm bells ought to have rung when the company's own president said it tasted 'like crap', yet the launch went ahead anyway. Sales failed to ignite and more than $300 million went up in smoke.

In his book on great marketing mistakes – *What Were They Thinking?* – marketing guru Robert McMath offers the following insights as to why the Premier smokeless cigarette failed:

- It tasted bad and smelled awful.
- It was designed to appeal to non-smokers, not the people who would actually buy it.
- It denied its users what McMath describes as 'a vapoury security blanket'.
- It was difficult to light and produced no ash, which denied smokers the ritual behaviour around disposing of it.

Was it a failure of technology or a failure to understand the consumer? If the technology could be improved, would the product sell?

McMath also blames office politics for the fact that so many products fail when they reach the market. Touching on many of the themes we've already encountered, he outlines several reasons why bad products survive to be launched:

- No one had the guts to say the idea was flawed (groupthink).
- A project gets approval because it can be done (technology for the sake of it).
- No one wants to be seen to miss an opportunity (hype and the 'better to try and fail' mentality).
- Innovators are afraid to admit they were over-optimistic about the project.
- It was the boss's pet project (ego involvement).

You can bet that the following lines of reasoning are also a one-way ticket to the 'pit of doom':

- 'I'll show them...'
- 'We've invested too much to give up now.'
- 'Let's press on with the launch and hope it all turns out well. If it fails we can blame the market or the marketing department and that won't look as bad as giving up now.'
- 'By the time the **** hits the fan I'll have found a new job.'

HOW MUCH DO WE *REALLY* LEARN FROM FAILURE?

The last of these options raises an interesting point: if you move on before the results of your errors become clear, how much have you learned from the experience? Weather forecasters learn very quickly when they make mistakes – they simply have to look outside the next day and compare reality with their predictions; then they can figure out where they went wrong in the first place.

But in business, the real outcome of decisions can take months, even years, to surface and it might be difficult to point to a specific reason for failure.

Indeed, many innovators may find it convenient to blame the market instead of their own failings. Others may choose not to dwell on their failures at all as they pick themselves up and move on to the next big venture. Nobody likes making mistakes, and everybody hates admitting to them.

Holding on to losers is a mistake that afflicts both innovators and investors, and for the same reason: it enables them to avoid the pain and regret of crystallizing a loss and leaves them with the hope that things will get better.

Psychologists Terry Odean and Brad Barber, respectively from The Haas School of Business at Berkeley and the University of California at Davis, have studied the behaviour of more than 60,000 investors in the US over several years. They found that our old friends overconfidence and over-optimism play a major part in the losing strategies of retail investors – both encourage them to trade too much, which reduces their returns because of transaction costs. But investors also hold on to losers when they should be ruthless and sell. Although it sounds like sentimental attachment, Odean says: 'It's more about avoiding regret. If you hold on to a loser you will always have the hope that it will bounce back and you'll be vindicated, but if you sell, not only do you have to face the fact that you've lost money, you'll also run the risk of seeing it bounce back after you've sold it.'

In the world of innovation, holding on to a project leaves you with the hope that the market will pick up and sales will take off. Sometimes they will, but more often than not, they won't. The bad thinking that leads you to hold on to a losing course of action is called 'escalation bias' and it will add significant losses to the ones you've already incurred in development. Research into escalation bias has highlighted factors such as ego involvement, self-justification and sunk costs as contributing factors. More recently, a study entitled *Stuck In The Past: Why organizations exhibit escalation bias* has offered a new insight into the problem. Authors Eyal Biyalagorsky, William Boulding and Richard Staelin, of Duke University, suggest that when considering new evidence – for example, market research – people have a tendency to overweight their previous opinions on the subject.

It works like this: the innovation process involves an initial decision to go ahead with a project based on the available evidence; some time later, if new evidence comes in, a second decision is required to either continue with or kill the project. In an intriguing experiment the authors asked two groups of people to evaluate information relevant to the launch of a new product. One group was asked to take the role of product manager, while the other was asked merely to act as an independent observer and assess the product's likelihood of success. The initial information suggested that the project would be profitable and consequently both groups gave it the go-ahead.

'Innovators can become too emotionally involved in their creations. They are often unwilling to stop and walk away from a project, or they become blind to what's going on around them. They set off with a great idea and whether it's six months or six years later, something pops out; but in that time the market could have changed beyond recognition and they haven't been taking notice.'

Tim Jones
Principal, Innovaro

'The concept of sunk costs is understood in business, but to individual innovators it doesn't seem to count. If they have spent years on a project they will be damned if they give it up, so they'll spend more time and money and refuse to walk away.'

Steven Veldhoen
Partner, Booz Allen & Hamilton

Later, both groups were given new evidence that the product was likely to do so badly it would actually be more profitable to abandon it and sell the machinery involved. More than half of the product managers chose to continue, despite the poor forecasts, which confirms the idea that they had become ego-involved with the project and this had seduced them into taking an overly-optimistic view of its prospects. What was interesting, however, was that more than a third of the 'independent' evaluators also recommended continuing with the launch, even though they had no personal involvement in the product or its launch. They were not ego-involved with the product; they were ego-involved with their previous opinions. Because of this they overweighted the value of those earlier beliefs and selectively chose to discount new evidence that clashed with them.

THE MYTH OF 'FIRST MOVER ADVANTAGE'

'First mover advantage' was the mantra of the dotcom boom but it seduced many entrepreneurs into bad thinking strategies as they rushed to get to market. In the frenzy it was far too easy to say: 'We don't have time to do market research.' From those heady days, one comment stands out among all the interviews I conducted for my newspaper, *Sunday Business*. When I asked a venture capitalist what his main concern was about the companies he was funding, he replied: 'It's that they're not spending my money quickly enough.'

With advisers voicing concerns like that, it's understandable that so many dotcom entrepreneurs got caught up in the hype and went on such profligate spending sprees in the name of 'land grab' and 'brand building' – they *had* to, otherwise they might not have secured funding!

'Focusing on time to market is the wrong approach because it can be used as an excuse for not doing proper due diligence or research. More sophisticated organizations look at time to profit. Innovators think they need to rush ahead but it's far better to spend a few weeks doing a detailed market analysis. It will give you a clearer idea of the market opportunity and help you avoid a lot of problems later on.'

Tim Jones
Innovaro

The theory works if the new entrant can build high barriers to entry and there's little competition from established players, but for most internet companies that simply wasn't the case. The old economy dinosaurs may have been wrong-footed by the upstart entrepreneurs but they had much deeper pockets, real cash flows and the benefit of trusted brands. Internet companies had to pay a high price for brand recognition and trust building and ultimately, many of them failed because the cost of acquiring a customer was more money than the customer actually spent.

When the bubble burst, the mantras became 'best to market' or 'path to profitability' and for many internet business ideas the emptiness of first mover advantage was exposed. That's not to fault people for believing it was a pathway to success – it probably made perfect sense at the time, given the uncertainty of what was a rapidly shifting market and the advice of backers like the one quoted above.

In fact, one of the central messages of this book is that all our decisions make sense to us at the time we make them and given the information we have to work with. The question we should ask is this: 'Are there different ways of thinking about what we want to achieve?'

In the case of first mover advantage, the idea had been seriously challenged at the start of the dotcom boom in a *Sloan Management Review* paper published in 1996 by Gerard Tellis and Peter Golder. Entitled *First To Market, First To Fail? Real causes of enduring market leadership*, it challenges the accepted wisdom that pioneers share the spoils of victory. Looking at 50 different categories the study found that:

- The failure rate of pioneers was 47%.
- Pioneers enjoyed a market share of just 10%.
- Pioneers were leaders in just 11% of the categories.

Arguing that it's better to be an early leader than a pioneer, Tellis and Golder identify five characteristics necessary for enduring market leadership:

- **Vision:** Can you define the way ahead?
- **Persistence:** Can you stay the course and fight off all challengers?

- **Commitment:** Can you deploy sufficient resources to the task ahead?
- **Innovation:** Can you innovate relentlessly and change when the market demands?
- **Asset leverage:** Can you redeploy your expertise into new markets?

In the world of technology it's not hard to see how a company such as Microsoft embodies all five characteristics. In almost all of its major product lines – its Windows operating system, its word processing and spreadsheet software and its Internet Explorer browser – Microsoft was most definitely *not* a pioneer. But now it just about owns the market for each.

The study concludes that being first to market provides more of an opportunity than an advantage:

'Without these factors, a first entrant is merely an alarm for competitors; by embodying these factors, a late entrant can outpace a lethargic pioneer. An earlier entry along with all the other factors is certainly an advantage. But being first to market by itself is neither necessary nor sufficient for enduring market leadership.'

'People who have innovative ideas often see a huge gap in the market and think: "Wow, if we can get in first and grab it we will do well." But what they don't often ask themselves is why there is a gap in the market? It might be there for a very good reason – there is no market.'

Dr Sue Eccles
Lecturer in Marketing, University of Lancaster

IDEAS FOR INNOVATORS

- If successful innovation is a matter of time, place, context and price, what makes a bad idea?
- As an innovator, how typical are you of your intended customers?

- How do you know what people want from your innovation – have you asked them, or are you projecting your own needs and desires on to them?
- What problems could overconfidence pose in your organization? How can you overcome them?
- How ego-involved are you with your innovation or your business? What problems could this create?
- What symptoms of groupthink can you detect in your organization? Why have they arisen and what can you do about it?
- How can you make constructive feedback a part of the innovation process?
- If someone gave you negative feedback regarding your innovation, would you listen to it or ignore it?
- Is it better to fail in the market or to give up before you get there? Are you ruthless enough to kill your own pet project?

7

Understanding the customer

'Customers buy products for many reasons, not necessarily the ones the product developers care about. Exciting technology? Yawn. Great ease of use? Yawn.'

Don Norman
The Invisible Computer

By now it should be apparent that people can be utterly irrational when it comes to adopting innovations. It saves money! So what? It saves time! So what? It will save your life! So what?

When he wrote *Diffusion of Innovations*, Everett Rogers devoted several pages to what he called 'individual-blame bias' – the tendency to blame consumers for not getting with the programme. Do you recall the report on metrication from Chapter 1? The one that said:

'They did not grasp the advantages of the metric system and did not understand that it was a better system.'

The implication is clear – the laggards were at fault for their apathy; not the metric system itself or the decision to abandon, what was for most people, a perfectly workable system of weights and measures and replace it with something new.

'Everyone resists change; it's a fundamental part of the human condition. People will change only when there's a significant advantage to them. If they believe the innovation offers a real benefit, they will adopt it.'

Colin Burns
Ideo London

Like the people who developed the metric system in the hope of making life easier for everyone, you've developed an innovative product, service or idea in the honest and well-intentioned belief that it will make people's lives easier, better or more fruitful. Then the ungrateful SOBs repay your vision and hard work by ignoring it! What is wrong with them? Don't they *get it*?

Maybe the question should be: What's wrong with *you*? What faulty assumptions might you be making about the people for whom the innovation is intended? The most dangerous assumption about any innovation is to think that it's so compelling it will sell itself. You may think it is, but the harsh fact of life is that your opinion counts for very little. If the potential user base doesn't buy into the big idea, you're in big trouble.

The problem is that people can find so many vague and woolly reasons *not* to adopt something new. These 'Nebulous Resistance Factors' include:

- 'I can't be bothered.'
- 'It's too fiddly.'
- 'What's the point?'
- 'I'm fine as I am.'

They will hang on to old habits, old ways of working, things that seem inefficient and out of date because they simply aren't motivated enough to change.

'"I can't be bothered" is an umbrella for a wide variety of factors that will differ from person to person. In the case of online shopping it might be that they can't be bothered to buy the computer to go online, or that they can't be bothered to learn how to navigate the site, or they can't be bothered to wait for the delivery. Innovators need to figure out in advance all the different ways people can't be bothered and develop strategies to overcome these barriers to adoption.'

Rudy Ruggles
Head of Innovation Research
Cap Gemini Ernst & Young: Centre for Business Innovation

People's resistance to change has been neatly captured in an equation attributed to the economist David Gleicher.

Gleicher's Formula for Change states that change will occur only if:

$$D \times V \times F > R$$

Where D = dissatisfaction with the way things are
               V = vision of what might be possible if things change
               F = the first steps that people can take to make the change
               R = resistance to change (in time, money or discomfort)

It's easy to see from this equation that if there is no dissatisfaction with the way things are (D = zero), resistance to change will not be overcome. The metric system is a good example of a situation where there is little or no dissatisfaction with the old way of measuring things, which is why people are reluctant to change.

Online grocery shopping is another good example. If anything is ripe for change it's the experience of fighting through the crowds on a Saturday morning with a couple of bored kids in tow. You spend ages navigating the aisles, queue for an eternity at the till and then lug it all home in carrier bags that almost cut your hands in half. Yet the demise of WebVan shows that people are quite prepared to put up with the hassle of supermarket shopping instead of doing all of it online and then waiting for the goods to be delivered.

In this case there is little dissatisfaction (D is close to zero), and although people have seen what might be possible (V may be high) they have been reluctant to take the first steps towards change (F is close to zero).

For many people, when it comes to making the change to online grocery shopping,

$$\textbf{Resistance to change} > \textbf{D} \times \textbf{V} \times \textbf{F}$$

and so they drive to the shops and put up with all the inconvenience.

Rational behaviour?

- When making a cup of coffee, why do you fill a kettle and boil it when microwaving a cup of water is quicker and cheaper?
- How many CD players do you have in your living room? (Remember that computers, DVD players and games machines all play music CDs.) In fact, why do you have so many separate devices when your PC will play music, DVDs and games?
- If executives are so busy and under so much time pressure, why don't they jog, roller skate or use a micro-scooter around the office? Surely it would save them precious time?
- Why do you buy books and CDs online and yet go to the supermarket for larger and bulkier commodity goods such as washing powder, bottles of water, toilet rolls etc?
- How much discount on a cappuccino would tempt you to walk an extra 100 yards to buy it? 10%, 20%, 50%?
- Would you work from home if the technology enabled it? Would you let your staff?

If that seems irrational, it emphasizes the point that rationality is very much a personal construct. We all have our irrational little foibles and it's often these that scupper great ideas.

What's more, other factors come into play, like emotion, culture and habit. As anthropologist Professor Lucy Suchman of Lancaster University explains: 'It's not that people aren't rational, it's just that they have different rationalities. Not only do you have to understand those different rationalities, you also have to understand their relationship with whatever it is you're creating.'

THE IMPORTANCE OF UNDERSTANDING THE CONSUMER

It seems trite and rather obvious to argue that it's important to find out what potential users are like and what they want from an innovation, but as we've already learned, many projects have failed because this seemingly essential part of the innovation process was omitted or done badly.

In a white paper published by the innovation consultancy Strategyn, based in Lantana, Florida, Tony Ulwick and John A Eisenhauer make the following rather depressing observation about why market research is frequently lacking:

> 'Most companies simply do not have the information they need, at the time the information is needed, to determine whether or not a product concept will ultimately succeed or fail in the marketplace. Many firms believe the information needed to make such a determination either does not exist or cannot be captured, and therefore do not attempt to obtain it.'

The result, they argue, is that companies believe that market research cannot serve their needs and so take the view that failure is simply a business expense that cannot be avoided.

But a study published in the *Journal of Product Innovation Management* in July 1997 highlights the fact that good intelligence is the key to success in the market. Authors Brian Ottum and William Moore gathered information on 58 product launches – half of which failed – and found that in 80% of successful launches the product team had better than average market intelligence at its disposal during the product development process. Of the failures, 75% used less than average amounts of market information during the project.

Much market research focuses on the size of the potential market and an estimate of how big a slice the innovation can grab. But as most internet companies discovered to their cost, the timing of adoption is important because investment and revenues can become hopelessly mismatched. Remember that the five categories of adopters – from innovators to laggards – suggest that the innovation moves along a series of adopter comfort zones as time goes on. It reaches the innovators' comfort zone first, at which point they feel inclined to adopt it, even if it is buggy, expensive and prone to crashes. Later adopters have different criteria – lower cost, greater reliability, greater social acceptance – and so the innovation must enter the later comfort zones with these new characteristics firmly attached.

Another point to bear in mind is that for every adopter there is an 'adoption decision' process that consists of the following phases:

- awareness of the problem or desire
- awareness of the innovation
- interest in the innovation (the 'so what?' factor)
- persuasion and the decision to adopt
- confirmation and retention.

It begins with the awareness that there is a problem and that there is an innovation to solve it. Likewise for wants and needs to be fulfilled (although in Western society most things are wants rather than needs). Therefore, the first question to ask of any innovation is not so much: 'What problem does this solve?' as 'Do people think there is a problem?' With innovations such as the metric system or online supermarkets, it's clear that many people don't think there is a problem with the way they do things now. The next questions might be: 'At what point would this *become* a problem?' or 'What would motivate you to change?'

In the case of wants there is an argument that entirely new classes of product can create desires that people didn't previously know they had. But do they really, or do they merely introduce a new context for existing desires? The Sony Walkman didn't create a desire to listen to music; the internet didn't create a desire for information. What was innovative about both was that they satisfied those existing desires in new ways.

In the persuasion phase it's important to remember that different adopters will have different criteria by which they will judge the innovation, as we'll see later in this chapter.

THE BASICS OF RESEARCH

Although there are many ways to find out what's important to consumers, from simple surveys to focus groups to hiring an anthropologist to live with the kind of people you're targeting (ethnography), there are some basic questions for which you need answers:

- What problem does the innovation solve and, more importantly, do people perceive it as a problem?
- What advantages will they perceive? (Not what advantages do *you* think it offers!)
- What will influence them to adopt the innovation? Education? Marketing? Peer pressure? How can you influence these and who will bear the cost?
- Will consumers think the benefits of the innovation worth the cost and effort of adopting it?
- Are they locked into existing ways of doing things, perhaps emotionally, financially, contractually or by training?
- Does the innovation require a change in the behaviour of users? If so, how will you get them to change? (You can't just trot out that corporate cliche 'we think the benefits are so compelling...')
- Does the innovation go against social or cultural norms or practices?
- Is the innovation unique or can rivals copy it easily? How will you respond to rivals?

● What value will each category of adopter put on the product/service?
● What new uses will people find for it? (There are people who use Apple's iPod MP3 player as a phone book and diary!)
● How quickly will the innovation reach the laggards in your market? How can you speed up the process?

If you're a potential investor or a market forecaster you also need to ask questions of consumers and whether they will adopt the innovation; sometimes you may have to think creatively about the kinds of questions you should be asking. Settling for a projection supplied by the company won't give you that extra bit of insight you need – don't forget that innovators and forecasters tend to be overly optimistic about growth markets.

In the case of online grocery shopping, for example, it might be important to know who is responsible for doing the weekly shopping and what access they have to the computer. Put in simplistic terms, if mum normally does the shopping but the computer is in dad's study or the son's bedroom, how will she feel about invading their territory and using their technology? What if she doesn't like using the computer? What if she enjoys going to the supermarket? Another example might be the idea of offering films over mobile phones – something Nokia's TV commercials have been telling us will soon be possible. In a case like this, you might want to find out whether people want to watch films while they're travelling, how long is their typical journey, what would motivate them to watch a film on a mobile device with a small screen.

Questions like these may seem like nit picking but they're *real world* issues that will affect the uptake of the innovation you're studying.

PERCEIVING THE INNOVATION

Back in Chapter 3 we looked at the many different characteristics by which an innovation is judged. But it's important to understand that those characteristics by themselves are not what matters – it's the adopter's perception of those characteristics and their relative importance to the adopter that really count.

The P3 model – Power, Performance and Perception

The P3 model of user attitudes towards innovation was developed by Andrew Dillon, of the University of Texas, and Michael Morris, of the Air Force Institute of Technology – both experts in human-computer interaction. They distinguished between the capabilities of the innovation and the user's perception of it and developed a model consisting of the three components that will drive its adoption:

- **Power:** An objective measure of what the innovation can actually do. Is it up to the task in hand?
- **Performance:** A measure of how users actually get along with it – for example, how easy do they find it, how many of its features do they use?
- **Perception:** Given the innovation's power and their own performance with it, do users think they should adopt it?

Note that the user's perception of power and performance is what counts, not the objective facts. The innovation may be up to the task but for some reason the user may decide it isn't. All three facets must be measured if the adoption process is to be understood properly.

Remember that the characteristics and competencies of adopters themselves will influence their attitudes towards the innovation. A competent touch typist might not feel any need to switch to voice recognition software; a geeky teenager and a technologically backward executive will have different requirements when it comes to choosing the latest wireless internet device (see table overleaf). For the teenager, style may be more important than technology; the executive may value ease of use and compatibility with desktop systems.

Relative importance of the characteristics of a wireless internet device

Characteristic	Ideal state	Importance of ideal state to	
		Geeky teenager	Befuddled executive
Cost	Low	High	Low
Complexity	Low	Low	High
Image	Good	High	Low
Compatibility	High	Low	High
Capability	High	High	High

Bear in mind that the perception of an innovation and its features can change with time. As time goes on, several things may happen that could influence a potential adopter:

- Economic factors may make it more or less appealing.
- The consumer's financial circumstances may change (so that higher cost becomes less or more important).
- A standards war may be resolved.
- The consumer's willingness to adopt innovations may change.
- The product may become cheaper, more reliable and easier to use.
- The consumer's peers have adopted the innovation and so a critical mass is reached that triggers their own decision to adopt.
- Social and political pressures may influence adoption, for example when Coca-Cola introduced New Coke and a bandwagon began to roll against it.

It's worth noting that the characteristics in the table above and the others listed in Chapter 3 are ones that have been identified by researchers studying how innovations take off. Consumers may have a different set of criteria that may not be fully explored if market researchers confine them to a particular set of characteristics.

Imagine the list above being applied to the Segway Human Transporter we encountered in Chapter 5, but with one omission – image. You might find that people were positive towards the machine in terms of its cost, ease of use, compatibility with existing transport systems and its technical capability. But if you don't ask them 'Would you feel stupid riding this?' you'd be missing an important factor affecting its uptake in the market. How people will feel riding the Segway is determined by their perceptions of themselves and others that might be using it:

- I would look stupid/cool on it
- That guy looks stupid/cool on it
- Wow, that cool guy on TV has one
- Oh dear, the dork on the help desk has one
- Everyone else is riding them so I won't look as foolish
- Everyone else is riding them so I'll look like a sheep if I get one
- Oh no, the police are using them
- I'll get one if my mates do
- Look at those bozos walking
- This is fun!

The Segway may be a clever piece of technology that saves you the bother of walking, but when people come to evaluate it it's a fair bet that factors like these will feature pretty high up in their adoption decision processes (not to mention the fact that the $5,000 it costs would buy you several alternative methods of transport!). But if you wanted to invest in the company or forecast its success, and you haven't given serious consideration to the question of rider image, you may not have been asking the right questions.

WHAT QUESTIONS TO ASK?

An interesting approach to finding out what are the right questions to ask has been proposed by Cherilyn Randolph of the University of Western Australia. In a paper entitled *Why Do We Hate Microsoft And Still Use Word?* she suggests that the first stage of research should be to elicit from consumers themselves what criteria are important, rather than impose on them a list of features in a questionnaire. Using a long list of words such as 'better, latest, belief, status symbol, toy, forced, masculine, frustrating, foolish' and many others, she argues that consumers will pick out the concepts most relevant to their adoption decision process. The next stage is to find out the relative importance of each notion to a variety of consumers to build up a picture of what will go through their minds when they evaluate the innovation. This, in turn, should guide market researchers into asking the most pertinent questions. It will also transform the research exercise from being led by innovators and their perceptions of what consumers want, to being more of an understanding about what consumers *really* want. The idea echoes Neil Rackham's findings in Chapter 4 that sales people should ask questions, not push features.

It's important to remember that, for any given set of features of an innovation, people will trade-off and compromise. For example, a number of businesses have started beaming money-off coupons to mobile phones as people pass near particular shops. The compromise in this case is this: 'Is it worth going out of my way to get a discount?' If you're a cash-rich, time-poor executive then 10% off a latte is unlikely to appeal if you have to spend 10 minutes walking to cash in the coupon. You'd rather pay the full price and get one now.

LOOKING FOR CLUES

Funnily enough, a lot of business ideas based on discount models like these appeared in an era when the phrase 'cash-rich, time-poor' was being bandied about quite a bit – implying that for a lot of people, time was more valuable than money. How many of the discount dotcommers spotted *that* little 'environmental clue' before discounting their way to the 'pit of doom'?

Environmental clues

Even if you're developing something new to the world, there may be clues in the environment that can give you some indication of how people might react. For example:

- **News by wireless internet:** This assumes people want news when they're out and about. How many people do you see clutching radios to their ears to stay in touch? How many people sign up for specialist alert services, such as football scores via SMS?
- **The Segway Human Transporter:** How many people use micro-scooters or Go-Peds to get around?
- **TV via mobile phone:** How many people do you see watching Casio pocket TVs?
- **Email in your car, accessed by speech recognition:** There is already concern that mobile phone use increases the risk of accidents.
- **Video clips via cash machines so you can see film previews and book tickets:** Have you noticed how people hate queuing at ATMs? Will they appreciate waiting even longer while the guy in front watches a trailer?
- **Avatar-based conferencing for business:** Ever noticed that executives think videoconferencing is a poor substitute for real meetings?
- **Microwave with an internet screen:** Are microwaves usually situated in places where eye-level use is convenient?
- **Hot desking:** Have you been to a conference or meeting and noticed that people almost invariably return to the same seat for each session, even if they didn't leave their stuff there during the break? What does that suggest?
- **The internet is the death of high street shopping:** At the same time as the internet has grown, so have high street coffee shops, suggesting that shopping is a leisure activity, not just a series of transactions.

Remember that these are just clues, but they can be a useful guide to how people might respond to an innovative new idea. You need to ask them why they are resisting what's already out there and how you can offer them a better alternative. In the case of pocket TVs, it may be that they are too bulky and have a poor battery life, not that people *don't* want to watch TV on a mobile device. Sending TV to a device they already carry, such as a phone, might open up new possibilities. You'd also need to understand the social aspects of watching TV while out and about. Maybe there's some kind of stigma attached to it? Maybe people will watch one kind of TV but not another; clips of Manchester United's latest goals might sell, soap operas might not.

WHAT MARKET RESEARCH *DOESN'T* TELL YOU

Innovations can fail even with the best market research, and, sometimes, great products can emerge without it – but that's no excuse for ignoring it completely.

The case of New Coke shows that even when a company launches an innovative new product based on extensive market research sometimes the response isn't what was expected. Although Coca-Cola knew that a fraction of its existing customers would be upset by the disappearance of the old, established drink and its replacement with New Coke, they felt it was a risk worth taking. What the company didn't foresee was the influence those discontented drinkers would have on other people and their decision to adopt New Coke. The loss of a national treasure was too much for Americans to bear.

The pitfalls of market research

- People can tell you what they think you want to hear.
- People will tell you price is important, but will often make trade-offs on price for other factors such as convenience or reliability. Many dotcom entrepreneurs failed to realize this and discounted too heavily.
- Too many customer opinions can lead to 'featuritis'. Sometimes gut feeling and judgement need to override what the research says. A good example is Palm Computing, which has resisted the temptation to add cool new features to its handheld computers, in order to keep them simple to use.
- Can people really tell you what they want if they don't know it exists?

- People may not be able to verbalize their problems or needs, which is why many companies hire ethnographers to watch them and film how they behave.
- The methodology can be inappropriate – a survey won't tell you how people grapple with technology when they come to use it.

Likewise, British Airways' decision to rebrand itself with its World Colours was based on extensive research with passengers, of whom 60% came from outside the United Kingdom. The problem was that in its heartland, BA's British customers didn't warm to the colourful new designs, nor did Britain's savage and influential press.

Another failure of innovation (despite masses of market research) was Purple Moon, an American software company that was launched in 1996 with the laudable intention of producing more compelling computer games for girls. Backed by Microsoft founder Paul Allen, Purple Moon's business was grounded on four years of market research into what girls wanted from computer games. While rival companies such as Mattel produced games like *Barbie Fashion Designer* that pandered to a stereotypical image of young girls' fascination for clothes and make-up, Purple Moon developed games that were more like stories with appealing characters. One such character was Rockett Movado, a sparky eighth-grader who starred in games such as *Rockett's New School*, in which her aim was to develop relationships within the cliques and classes of high school.

For all its research and some very innovative products, Purple Moon closed its doors in February 1999, blaming intense competition from rivals such as Mattel for its demise. It seems the girls preferred Barbie to Rockett.

INNOVATION'S 'BEHAVIOURAL PREMISES'

Was Purple Moon's demise solely down to competition, or was it making faulty assumptions about the behaviour of its target market, despite all the research it collected?

Professor Randall Schultz, whose ideas on ego involvement we encountered in the last chapter, has also developed some thought provoking ideas about the adoption of new products. His notion of 'Behavioural Premises' is a useful way to challenge the assumptions that innovators are making about the consumer.

Schultz says: 'Every time you hear about a new product or a marketing plan you should step back and ask yourself what assumptions are being made about human behaviour.' Noting that the failure rate for new products remains so high, Schultz criticizes many marketing plans for being 'out of touch with reality' and questions whether product developers and marketing teams sit down and debate the underlying assumptions they are making about the behaviour of their target customers.

He describes a Behavioural Premise as:

'An assumption about consumer behaviour in the target market, stated in such a way that if that assumption is wrong the product will probably fail.'

Think of it as an elevator pitch to a venture capitalist who's going to the first floor! In effect, it's about sitting down and asking: 'Is this really how people will behave in the real world?' The point is it can and *should* be done long before the product ever reaches the market.

Schultz cites the example of Purple Moon's computer game *Rockett's New School* as a product with a dubious Behavioural Premise. 'They decided to launch the product by telling young girls aged 8–12 that they could play this game and simulate real-life experiences, such as having to move to a new school and make new friends. But what can be more stressful for a young girl than having to leave all her friends behind, go somewhere new and start all over again making new friends? The Behavioural Premise here is that young girls want to simulate stressful situations when they play and immediately it sounds ridiculous.'

It's worth looking at the Behavioural Premises behind some other ideas; remember that the issue is not whether *some* people will behave in this way, it's whether *enough* people will to create a profitable market and justify the investment. Consider the following Behavioural Premises:

- **Male contraceptive plug:** Men will jam a plug into the most sensitive part of their anatomy and lock it there before indulging in a pleasurable sexual experience.
- **Avatar-based conferencing for business:** Executives will use something that resembles a computer game to conduct important business discussions, instead of meeting face to face, using the telephone, email or videoconferencing.
- **Mobile commerce:** When out and about, people's desire to shop is so great that they will do so using a small screen, low resolution device instead of visiting a real shop or waiting until they reach a better internet terminal.
- **Location-based money-off coupons sent by Short Message Service (SMS):** People will go out of their way to get a discount on something they might not previously have thought of buying.
- **Films on your mobile phone:** When travelling, people will pay a premium to watch a film on a device with a tiny screen.
- **Augmented visual reality:** People are unhappy with the information content of the real world and want additional information beamed into their eyes.
- **Personal bar code scanners that link information on paper to websites:** People cannot be bothered to type a URL into a computer and will prefer to scan a bar code instead, either by taking the bar code to the computer or by scanning it with a mobile device and then uploading it to the computer.
- **Boo.com:** People will forego trying on clothes before buying them; instead they will order them online, wait a few days and then try them on, risking the inconvenience of having to return them if they are not right.
- **LetsBuyIt.com:** In return for a discount, people will wait up to three weeks to receive goods they have ordered through an online buying collective.

Although some Behavioural Premises throw up clear losers, like the male contraceptive plug, others need a bit more thought – but they provide an excellent starting point for debate.

But remember that a Behavioural Premise is an assumption about the behaviour of consumers in a particular niche. Avatars may not make it in the business arena but they are hugely popular in online computer games like *EverQuest* and have allowed people to virtually 'attend' sci-fi conferences. Boo.com's model may have failed but catalogue shopping has been around for ages and it's based on almost exactly the same premise. Augmented reality may sound like technology gone mad for most people, but for a 747 mechanic it might replace a bulky set of manuals and make the maintenance process a lot more efficient. All of this just goes to prove the point that maybe there really *aren't* any bad innovations (contraceptive plugs apart), there are just bad contexts for otherwise good ideas.

CULTURAL DIFFERENCES

The success of innovations is not only a function of perception and time, it is also a function of geography and culture. What works in one country might not work in another – one of the best examples being the use of condoms in catholic countries. They may be a truly great innovation, but if *il Papa* says it's wrong, their adoption and use is likely to be resisted.

Even with innovations that don't foster religious controversy, cultures that are broadly similar can react in markedly different ways. In the UK, for example, people view city centre surveillance cameras as a positive and largely benign development in the fight against crime and disorder. In the US, however, they are regarded with suspicion and outright hostility, because Americans take the issue of 'privacy' much more seriously (although they do seem to have an unhealthy appetite for 'reality' TV programmes made from footage shot by surveillance cameras!).

The Brits also have a love affair with text messaging, sending more than a billion messages a month via SMS, whereas most Americans prefer to talk on their mobile phones and consider SMS rather quaint! Europe as a whole has a greater uptake of cell phones than the US because the entire continent – and most of the rest of the world – has standardized around GSM. Meanwhile, in Japan, the iMode wireless mobile phone and internet service is hugely popular – probably because home computer penetration is much lower in

Japan and the Japanese spend much longer commuting on public transport. In the US, by contrast, home PCs are far more ubiquitous and most people drive to work, so the innovation of iMode may not find a market there.

Another intriguing example of a vast cultural chasm can be found at the breakfast table, according to Professor Basil Englis of Berry College in Georgia. An expert in market research, Professor Englis studied the breakfast habits of Scandinavians on behalf of a cereal manufacturer and found some surprising differences. 'It's important to realize that there is a strong cultural context to breakfast,' he explains of his research. 'If you're trying to sell breakfast cereal that you serve with cold milk, you may have problems because you're violating a cultural tradition, which is to serve a typically Scandinavian meal of bread and cheese in the morning.' Breakfast cereal may be convenient and quick to prepare, and it may be just as good in nutritional terms, but Scandinavian parents have grown up with the idea of nurturing their children in a different way – by serving them a breakfast that is 'culturally situated'. They might not feel good about serving cold cereal for breakfast; they might even feel that they were somehow neglecting their children by doing so.

Professor Englis also notes that innovators often overlook cultural factors in their own backyards: 'There's a strong cultural tradition being lost in online shopping and I don't think internet companies have paid enough attention to that,' he explains. 'When you go out and buy things there's a tremendous amount of social interaction going on, even if it's only between you and the salesman – even if it's short-lived, it's still a relationship.'

GM Food – Have *both* sides made faulty assumptions about consumer behaviour?

Genetically modified (GM) food is an innovation that has yet to gain widespread acceptance in the market, especially in countries like Britain where opposition has been both fierce and vocal. The spectre of 'Frankenstein food' has led consumers to resist even the most basic GM products such as tomato paste and soya, but supporters argue that it could help to feed the poor and reduce the need for expensive and damaging agrichemicals.

However smart and compelling an idea GM food is, and however safe it may be, this is clearly an innovation where consumer perception counts for far more than objective scientific reality.

On the consumer side the important characteristics seem to be image, risk and social acceptance, whereas the producers of GM food are promoting benefits such as quality, cost and taste. It's worth considering that these same characteristics are the ones that have played an important role in the poor performance so far of many online grocery stores; customers rate quality, cost and taste so highly that they're reluctant to trust the job of selecting fresh produce to pickers (though they might trust them to select more standard items like tins of tomatoes, kitchen rolls etc). In the case of GM food, however, a different set of characteristics becomes uppermost in their adoption decision process.

Both sides of the GM argument think it's important to educate the market in order to influence their adoption decisions, but have they been making the right assumptions about what is important to consumers? According to a couple of marketing experts at the University of Illinois, the answer is no.

Professor Brian Wansink and graduate student Junyong Kim argue that both the producers and opponents of GM food have fundamentally misunderstood what is going on in the minds of potential adopters and this has led to poor campaigns on both sides.

In a paper published in the journal *American Behavioral Scientist* in 2001, they argue that because most people lack the scientific knowledge or the motivation to evaluate the benefits and risks of GM food directly, they rely on peripheral routes to persuasion, such as news reports, expert opinions, advertising, public opinion and campaigning.

The authors outline several mistaken assumptions they believe the supporters and opponents of GM food are making.

The mistaken assumptions of supporters:

- **The GM issue will blow over:** In effect they are exhibiting a pro-innovation bias typical of many other technologists in believing that progress is inevitable and that consumers will eventually come round to their way of thinking and recognize the benefits of GM food. It didn't happen that way with nuclear power!
- **When people have the facts, they will make the 'right' decision:** Unfortunately, most people probably can't evaluate the 'facts' properly and so they are more likely to be influenced by sound bites. It also assumes consumers make rational decisions based on objective evidence and that all consumers will weight each piece of evidence the same way. But as we've already seen, different characteristics will influence adopters in different ways. Good taste may be less important than perceived risks.
- **GM food is really an industry issue:** Wrong – it's a consumer perception issue that needs to be addressed by good branding and marketing to create a more positive attitude towards GM food. At present, consumers regard consumer groups as being more trustworthy sources of information than GM food producers and government.
- **GM is just another branch of biotechnology that consumers have already accepted in medicines, so they ought to accept it in food:** Medicine saves lives whereas good food merely promotes health, and so people perceive biotech medicine as reducing losses, which is a concept to which most people can relate. Even if they are opposed to biotechnology, the chances are they would risk it if the alternative was serious ill health. GM food doesn't have such obvious benefits, because most good foods will promote health, not just GM. Why bother adopting GM – with whatever risks are perceived – if the benefits are not significantly greater than for eating normal food?

The mistaken assumptions of opponents:

- **People want to be informed:** This is like the rather dubious assumption that people want to be connected to the internet all the time. However, as Wansink and Kim point out, more people watch sitcoms and soaps than watch the news and most people simply can't be bothered to gather and absorb all the evidence they would need to make an informed decision.
- **People need to be informed:** Because consumers are neither motivated nor scientifically knowledgeable enough to evaluate all the information on GM food, they are happy to sub-contract the decision-making to outside agencies, such as America's Food and Drug Administration (FDA). These outside agencies will in turn do the thinking for them and arrive at a sensible decision over safety. In short, if the FDA says it's safe, it's safe.
- **Changing consumer attitudes will change their behaviour:** Consumers may be against GM food but still eat it. Their attitude has remained the same, but they have voted with their stomachs! Some people resent information overload but still put up with hundreds of email messages every week.
- **The risks of the unknown are more important than the benefits:** Consumers will make trade-offs and may soften their stance against GM food if they see it as offering substantial benefits. For example, a GM food that requires no pesticides or fertilizers to grow may be regarded positively by many consumers, simply because they are more concerned about pesticide pollution than about the potential risks of biotechnology. A better tasting tomato may not appeal to them if it is genetically modified.

(Source: Wansink, Brian and Junyong, Kim. *The Marketing Battle Over Genetically Modified Foods: False assumptions about consumer behavior, American Behavioral Scientist*, 44: 8 (April 2001), 1405–17.)

IDEAS FOR INNOVATORS

- Think of five reasons why people can't be bothered to adopt your innovation. Now develop strategies to overcome their resistance (and try to do it without using the words 'price', 'features' or 'compelling').
- Do you have better than average information about your target market? If not, why not?
- List five reasons for *not* conducting a thorough market analysis. For each argument, find a rebuttal.
- Look back at the 'adoption decision process' and, for each stage, develop three different strategies to increase your chances of success.
- Look back at the section headed 'The basics of research' and answer every question for your own innovation.
- Rate your innovation on the P3 model of Power, Performance and Perception – you will need a user to do this.
- How will adopters' perceptions of your innovation change with time? What will change their perceptions?
- What kind of research is most appropriate for your innovation? Should you involve users in the early stages of its design? What problems could that generate?
- What is the Behavioural Premise behind your innovation? Write it down and see if it makes sense.
- How will different cultures perceive the innovation? Are there any cultural barriers to its adoption? (Think of selling condoms in the Vatican!)

8

The home of the future?

'Wouldn't it be helpful if the refrigerator could let you know when the milk had gone bad by sending a quick message across the bottom of your TV screen?'

Smart Computing, July 2000

Innovation in the home is a perennial favourite for what journalists call an 'ADLF' feature – a day in the life of the future – and no glimpse of the brighter world to come would be complete without the fully automated, constantly connected home in which everything talks to everything else and the robotic vacuum cleaner pootles around cleaning up when you've gone off to work.

The alarm clock emails the coffee machine to tell it to start brewing, while you make your way to the bathroom and brush your teeth in front of a mirror that doubles as a huge organizer screen, showing you your appointments for the day. Go downstairs and the internet-enabled microwave has downloaded a recipe for hash browns, checked with the fridge and ordered a couple of pints of milk which are on their way courtesy of the local instant delivery service. After watching the news on a screen placed conveniently on the refrigerator door, you can relax and read your overnight text messages, which have been burned on to your toast by the Bluetooth-enabled toaster. Your networked washing machine tells you it has downloaded the latest wash programme from technical support so now you can get your smalls even cleaner using *40 degree Ver. 1.05*, which is a big improvement on the old 40 degree cycle with which your previous and unconnected washing machine was lumbered.

Far from being a techno-utopian dream, all of these ideas were seriously touted at the height of the internet boom when the *zeitgeist* was 'network everything'. Domestic appliance manufacturers such as Whirlpool, Electrolux, Sunbeam, LG Electronics and Merloni unveiled ambitious plans to turn the dream of a networked home into an everyday reality.

Sensibly, however, many of their initiatives were actually research programmes designed to find out what customers really wanted from their home appliances. After all, white goods manufacturers are not impulsive start-ups that develop and launch products based on a founder's whim rather than on the findings of hard consumer research. Electrolux, for example, developed its famous ScreenFridge after extensive ethnographic research into the way people congregated in particular rooms of the house. It's now being tested with 50 families to see how they use it in real life.

Another manufacturer, Sunbeam, created a new division called Thalia to develop 'Thinking and Linking Intelligent Appliances' including an alarm

> 'The role of technology within the kitchen is very different from the role of technology around the rest of the home. The kitchen is where we prepare food and so it has strong cultural roles that centre around nurturing, protection and cleanliness. Technology is usually quite dissonant with those roles because people perceive it as hard and alienating, particularly if it is connected technology. If you want to bring the internet into the kitchen you have to understand that what you're doing is bringing the whole world – good and bad – into this nurturing, protected environment and people may not think that's appropriate. Focusing on the technology and how it is used is wrong – you should focus on the people and how they live their lives.'
>
> Nick Jankel-Elliott
> Ethnographer, Happy Dog Group

clock, coffee maker, electric blanket and a smoke alarm. At the time of Thalia's launch in the spring of 2000, Sunbeam chief executive Jerry Levin commented: 'Sunbeam is the natural leader to implement whole house connectivity.' But less than two years later, in August 2001, the division was closed and Sunbeam abandoned the idea of developing a proprietary system of linking appliances together using power line technology.

The reasons for Thalia's demise were signalled a few months earlier when chief executive Gwen Wisler spoke to *mpulse*, a magazine produced by Hewlett Packard's 'Cooltown' project (which is also devoted to this notion of 'pervasive' computing):

'What we kept hearing from consumers was that we, the manufacturers, were making products more complicated than they needed to be. The products we were trying to push, they didn't necessarily want.'[1]

So it seems the idea of networked appliances is one that, for the time being, appeals more to technologists than consumers. The arguments for using networked appliances are worth analyzing because many of the underlying ideas are more sensible than people think – it's just that the home may not be the best market for such innovative thinking.

ANY OLD IRON?

One of the strangest ideas around in the heady days of the internet boom was a suggestion that irons could be fitted with Bluetooth chips so their owners could check if they'd remembered to switch them off before leaving for work. It's an intriguing notion – how many times have you experienced that nagging doubt and even had to rush back and check?

But is a complex technological solution involving Bluetooth and the internet really the best way to alleviate your concerns? What would it take to achieve it? A Bluetooth chip, a sensor to tell if the iron was still on, a receiver of some kind in the kitchen through which the iron could communicate, a link to the internet, some means of identifying an individual iron, maybe on a home page where you could monitor the status of every connected device in your home, and of course a way for you to turn the thing off remotely.

If it sounds like technology for the sake of it, it probably is – especially when manufacturers could simply fit a timer switch that automatically turned the darn thing off if it hadn't been picked up for five minutes. But safe thinking like that isn't exactly capturing the spirit of the age is it? Nor does it attract the attention of journalists.

EMAIL IS TOAST

Another mad idea is the Bluetooth-enabled toaster that burns messages into your toast every morning. If it sounds ridiculous, check out the book *Being Digital* by Professor Nicholas Negroponte, head of the Media Lab at the Massachusetts Institute of Technology. Back in 1995 he said:

> 'A toaster should not (just) be able to burn toast. It should be able to talk to other appliances. It would really be quite simple to brand your toast in the morning with the closing price of your favourite stock. But first, the toaster needs to be connected to the news.'[2]

The professor doesn't explain *why* the toaster needs to be connected to the news but argues that:

> 'The lack of electronic communication among appliances results in, among other things, very primitive and peculiar interfaces in each.'

I've no idea what kind of Heath-Robinson device Professor Negroponte uses to toast his bread in the morning, but the interface on mine consists of a simple dial numbered 1–6 and a push-down mechanism to start it off. It's primitive, but it works. Does a toaster really need to be any more complicated than that? What possible value would it add to our experience of eating toast for breakfast? Indeed, does it need to be any *less* complicated – perhaps by adding a voice recognition system so we're spared the drudge of turning the dial? Would that improve it? Why on earth does a simple toaster need to be turned into some kind of networked information device to satiate our demand for connectivity – or at least what technologists *believe* to be our demand for connectivity?

Professor Negroponte's engaging idea was actually turned into a real toaster as a graduation project by a student at one of the UK's design colleges. What was surprising was that it attracted nearly 600 words of uncritical puff on the BBC's News Online website, which just goes to show that technology journalism in the mainstream media is all about entertainment, not critical analysis.

The networked toaster may just be an amusing example designed to illustrate what is possible, but behind it is the belief – usually touted by computer and networking companies keen to open up new markets – that our lives will surely improve if we connect everything to the net. But why complicate simple, inexpensive appliances that are already good enough for our needs?

THE INTERNET MICROWAVE – FOR SO MUCH MORE THAN ZAPPING READY MEALS

Another smart appliance that was being shown off during the bubble was the intelligent networked microwave. One of the common arguments for this is that it will cook your ready meals to perfection by following instructions sent to it by a chip on the packaging. Given that some microwaves are as confusing to programme as video recorders, it sounds like a good idea. But in the real world, how do we actually use our microwave ovens? The majority of us don't really cook with them, we just bung in curries and zap them on 'high' for a few minutes until they're bubbling. Most of us have little need for low, medium and defrost, and I doubt that many microwaves ever run for more than ten minutes at a time, let alone cook joints of beef or chickens. That's the reality of how most microwaves are used – they heat ready meals. Would precision timing really improve the experience of heating and then eating a Chicken Tikka Masala? Should we all foot the bill for installing radio tags on to packaging just to cook it precisely to the second, or is the process we use today perfectly good for our needs?

Of course, radio tags on packaging may take over from bar codes as a means of controlling inventory in the supermarket, in which case the cost of adding some extra information about cooking times may be negligible and the economics and rationale of the idea may become more compelling. But is it really such a drudge to read the instructions and turn the dials to 'high' and '3 minutes'? Is the experience so problematical that it needs to be 'simplified' by adding more technology? Remember that the ready meals industry is driving towards simpler meals that don't require the whole gamut of microwave programmes to cook. Anyway, what cost-benefit analysis would justify such a development that, at best, would free up an extra two seconds of our time?

Another common justification for the networked microwave (and networked cooking appliances in general) is that we'll all be able to download recipes from the internet. The BBC puts lots of recipes on to the websites that support its seemingly endless cookery programmes, but again, in the real world, how many of us actually bother with them? A survey commissioned by the oven chip manufacturer McCain (published by NOP in March 2002) revealed that the average British kitchen contains 1,000 recipes in various cookbooks, but the average cook uses just seven of those recipes every year!

There's the paradox – we love to buy cookbooks, but rarely do we do anything more than browse through them and drool over the pictures. But, no one in their right mind would argue that we should stop producing cookbooks simply because people don't use them. In our glorious, irrational ways, we think nothing of forking out £15 for the latest book from our favourite celebrity chef, but if you planned to charge £15 a year so that people could access thousands of recipes on a website, and gave them the added value of a database that could suggest ideas and dinner party menus, I doubt you'd get even ten seconds of a venture capitalist's time. It's a great idea, but so what?

Another finding from the NOP survey was that most people regarded most kitchen gadgetry as rather pointless – the blowtorch being cited by

83% of respondents as the most useless gadget, and a surprising 63% saying pretty much the same about coffee grinders. More than 60% of Brits have seven or more spice jars in the rack, but only three have ever been used more than once. Will people find an internet-enabled microwave more useful than a coffee grinder?

In 2000, the US embedded chip manufacturer Lantronix demonstrated an internet-enabled barbecue grill so that anyone with a web browser could check the temperature of the grill and the meat from anywhere in the world. How useful.

40 DEGREES VERSION 1.05

The networked kitchen of the future wouldn't be complete without an internet-enabled washing machine like the Ariston Margherita2000, which the company unveiled in 2000 as part of its expansion into digital devices. (Other products announced at the time included a wired oven capable of downloading recipes and the correct programmes with which to heat them.)

Ariston's website explains some of the benefits of networking devices such as ovens and washing machines:

- It allows HQ to monitor their performance and diagnose any problems before they happen.
- They can regulate power consumption in the home so as not to cause an outage, and to optimize power consumption. In the event of a possible blackout they can decide whether to prioritize the washing machine or the oven.

Both are undoubtedly useful ideas that could be scuppered by the cost-benefit analysis of installing all the additional equipment needed to make it happen. Most homes have power supplies robust enough to survive several appliances being switched on at once and if they don't the residents will generally learn pretty quickly that you can't run the washing machine at the same time as the dryer (I speak from experience!). Does this really need the benefit of computer monitoring or can you crack the problem with a Post-It Note? A more sensible idea for networked power management is that in many countries power is cheaper at night and at certain times of the day. In the UK the pricing is fairly dynamic from day to day and hour to hour and a networked washing machine could check with the power company's website and decide when to turn itself on. Again, it's a smart idea that will doubtless face the 'so what?' factor when it comes to impressing consumers who might not be bothered with a device that could save just a few pennies here or there. They might not appreciate the spin cycle running at 3am either!

Another frequent justification for the networked washing machine is that it will be able to download the latest wash programmes to clean the clothes just right. Here again, a spot of real world observation might reveal that people only use a fraction of all the different wash cycles available to them. For most of us it's 60 degrees for whites and 40 degrees for everything else – and most of the time these basic programmes are good enough. Would version 1.05 of the 40-degree cycle really make any difference? Maybe it will: Zanussi, a division of Electrolux, is developing a smart washing machine that weighs the load, adds water, tests the absorbancy of the clothes and then decides how best to wash them. According to Electrolux vice president Tom Wells, the clever thing about this new machine is that it doesn't have any programmes at all – just an 'On' switch. Now *that's* progress; get the technology out of people's faces and hide it all away. But if it's even £50 more than a conventional washing machine, will people consider it worth the extra cost? Here again, it's a question of whether people think turning a dial is too much bother for them or whether the existing technology is good enough for their needs.

It turns out, however, that some people apparently *do* think turning a dial is too much effort. In April 2002 (and not on April Fool's Day) Electrolux launched what it claims is the first washing machine that talks. Aimed at the Indian market, the endearingly-named 'Washy Talky' tells the user what to do when loading the clothes: 'Open lid, add detergent, close lid'. The machine was developed after focus groups in India expressed the desire for something that explained all the procedures and could tell them when something was amiss. Apparently, Washy Talky's voice is that of a softly spoken, middle-class Indian woman who speaks both English and Hindi. Luckily, 'I'm afraid I can't do that, Dave' isn't in her vocabulary.

YOUR REFRIGERATOR IS PROBABLY NOT ABOUT TO BREAK DOWN

IBM used to run a TV commercial in which a maintenance engineer visits a home and informs the residents he's come to fix the refrigerator. Somewhat befuddled, the family tell him they haven't called for his services because the refrigerator isn't broken. 'Not yet,' he replies, 'it's about to.'

The commercial is designed to tell people how much brighter the future will be when our fridges can diagnose themselves and call for help when they need to. But like many of the examples that technologists give us to justify adding yet more technology to our lives, it's a terrible example!

The fact is that domestic refrigerators are incredibly reliable machines that set the standard for just about everything else we use in our daily lives. If computers were even 1% as reliable as fridges the world really *would* be a better place. In fact, in 2001, the manufacturer Frigidaire launched a quest to find the oldest Frigidaire still working in the US. The winner was built in 1923! According to Electrolux vice president Tom Wells, fridges are engineered for a long life: 'They're normally replaced after ten years or so, but we build them to last for a couple of decades at least.'

In fact, refrigerators would be even more reliable but for an innovation that failed back in the 1930s. Nowadays, all fridges have a series of pipes containing a coolant fluid that absorbs heat from the air in the fridge, cooling the interior down. An electric compressor condenses the liquid in a heat exchange at the back of the fridge and so heat from the fridge is transferred back into the kitchen. But in the 1930s a rival technology existed – the gas refrigerator – which had no moving parts to go wrong (in today's fridges the compressor is usually the thing that eventually breaks down). Instead, the gas fridge used a simple flame to heat an ammonium coolant that evaporated to produce a cooling effect.

Despite its apparent advantage over electric models, the potentially more reliable gas fridge failed as an innovation because of corporate vested interests. The likes of General Electric and Westinghouse were firmly in the electric camp and so they were not interested in developing the quieter and more efficient gas fridge. Their bigger R&D and marketing budgets are the reason that fridges make the humming noise they do today.

But as to the networked fridge the question is this: would adding diagnostics and networking infrastructure to a household refrigerator make it more reliable or less? The fridge in your kitchen can hum away for 20 years without needing to be rebooted. Can you say that of any networked or computing equipment around today? Maybe computer manufacturers and software companies should focus on making their products as reliable as fridges instead of lobbying to insert their own rather flaky technologies into other people's products under the spurious premise that they will somehow become more reliable!

Here's another interesting thought: if the networked fridge has the capability to email the service centre when it feels it's about to break down, what kind of message will it send? If you plug it in and it doesn't detect a problem for 20 years, will its cry for help be recognized when the time comes? Technology and protocols may move on and leave today's networked fridge in a time warp. Companies change and so do business models. In a few years time, the concept of the networked fridge may be regarded as just another interesting idea that wasn't commercially viable, so why bother supporting it any more?

Another supposedly compelling argument for the networked fridge is that it will take away the drudge of shopping for those essentials like milk and eggs. Add some kind of bar code scanner and the fridge will keep an inventory of its contents and reorder food when necessary. 'It will have a computer screen on the fridge door so you can see an inventory of what's inside,' gushed one enthusiast when I asked him what was the point. My response to this was that it would be a terrible shame for humanity to lose the ability to open a door, given that most of us master this skill at quite an early age.

Like other wired appliances, the networked fridge seems like a great idea until you give it half a minute's thought. Firstly, bar code or even radio tagged packages will tell the fridge what packages it contains, not what food is in them. A carton of milk can be empty or full and the fridge will be none the wiser. If the carton is taken out for a minute, does the fridge reorder immediately? Remember that a carton of milk will make several journeys between the fridge and the counter during its brief life; do you want to have to hit some kind of order override button every time you want to make a cup of tea? What if you don't want to reorder? Why add the extra fiddliness in order not to order?

'It will also let you log on to a website and check what's in your fridge,' my enthusiastic chum added. But let's think about this rationally: if you can't remember whether you have enough milk, why not just grab some on the way home? If you already had milk, you'll have more (which you can freeze); if you forget, it's no big deal. Is it really worth adding a bar code scanner, network infrastructure, software, hardware, web pages and everything else just to ensure you've got enough milk for a cup of tea? The idea of automatic food reordering mistakenly assumes that people are creatures of habit when it comes to eating, when in fact we are far more spontaneous. Other than milk, the things we *do* reorder time and time again are not usually the kinds of goods we store in fridges. It also presupposes that people consider grocery shopping to be a dreadful chore, which, as I'll argue later on in this book, is a rather dubious assumption that cost investors a lot of money when they backed a spectacular flop called WebVan.

Another use being touted for the networked fridge is that it can monitor the wellbeing of the people who use it, on the simple premise that if the fridge door hasn't been opened all day something is wrong. It's an innovative idea that obviously came from some clever lateral thinking. But it might not appeal to the people who most need it – the elderly and infirm. Somehow, I suspect they'd prefer to get help as soon as they feel ill, not hours later when the fridge thinks: 'Hang on, I haven't been opened all day; what's wrong?' Many companies already make simple help buttons to wear on the wrist or around the neck so that if the wearer collapses they can press the button and an automatic distress message is relayed by telephone to a help centre. It's not as sexy an idea as using internet technology to solve the problem, but I know which system I'd prefer.

The networked fridge – a false icon of the internet age?

Electrolux vice president Tom Wells describes the company's research into networked home appliances:

'The ScreenFridge evolved out of some research we did with a university in Sweden because we were trying to find out which rooms in the home people visited the most and whereabouts in the room they were. We found that the place they went to most often was the kitchen and much of the time they were close to the fridge, either walking past it or sitting nearby. That's why it has become the "communications hub" of the home – you'll often see pictures or messages stuck to it with fridge magnets.

We thought it would be an interesting experiment to update the fridge's role as communications hub by putting a screen on it and so we envisaged an appliance with internet access, radio, TV and some sort of food management system using bar codes so that the fridge would know what it contained and be able to reorder food over the internet.

The ScreenFridge was a concept, just to show what could be done with the technology. In fact, the bar code system isn't practical as yet because it tells you what packages are in the fridge, not what they contain. Maybe a more sophisticated system will come along in the future.

A lot of other manufacturers have brought out their own internet-enabled fridges and they've even gone as far as to develop internet-enabled washing machines and microwaves, but how many of them have stopped and asked themselves how useful any of this technology is to people?

There's a great temptation to say: "Look what we can do with the technology" but what you should be asking is: "What can technology do for the customer?" A lot of people have come into this field with all sorts of ideas about networking and gateways and portals, but they have been concentrating on technological possibilities, not customer needs. The mistake is to concentrate on the technology; the only way to succeed is to put the customer first, second, third and everywhere else. Electrolux isn't a technology company, we are a consumer goods company and what it boils down to is this: do real people have a real need for an internet-enabled fridge and will they pay real money for it?

We've put the ScreenFridge into a long-term trial with 50 families to find out exactly how they use it, what kind of surfing they do with it and find out about human factors such as how high the screen should be. As it stands, we don't think the ScreenFridge is desperately practical just yet. In a way, the networked fridge has become a false icon.'

ROBOVAC OR ROBOFLOP?

No house of the future would be complete without the robotic vacuum cleaner to take away the drudge of Hoovering (or should that be Dysoning?) the home. Indeed, Electrolux has already put its own version of the robotic vacuum on the market, a sweet little machine called the Trilobite, costing 1,500 euros – four times as much as a non-robotic Dyson!

The Trilobite uses ultrasound to navigate its way around the house. Unfortunately, it can't cope with stairs (a failing that scuppered the Daleks' plans for world domination in that sci-fi classic *Dr Who*), and owners have to pull up their carpets and place magnetic strips underneath to warn it of impending falls into the stairwell of doom. But the Trilobite's creators claim that it cleans more of the carpet than the average human, who misses some 30% of the dirt.

Electrolux claims it can cope with rugs, but can it cope with their stringy edges? As everyone knows, the stringy bits on the edges of rugs are the vacuum cleaner's nemesis. The only way to stop the poor machine choking is to step on the rug and hoick the cleaner sharply backwards. (Actually, my Dyson DC-05 has a clever button that opens a hole in the extension pipe, thus reducing suction in the cleaning head and releasing its grip on the rug, which shows a nice attention to detail on the part of Dyson's designers.)

The serious point about RoboVac is this: vacuuming is a tango for two. When we go around the house with our Dysons we grab things and move them to clean behind them, and when we're finished we have a clean room and a sense of achievement. RoboVac can't move the dining room chairs to vacuum under the table, so we'd still have to do that ourselves. If we have to clear away the 'rug of doom' and every other life-threatening piece of domestic flotsam before letting the little blighter loose, what real value has it added to the process of cleaning? We'd have already done most of the physical work of vacuuming.

There is another problem with RoboVacs – suction. Because conventional vacuum cleaners rely on humanity for a push, they can devote all their energy to what they do best – sucking up dirt. The Trilobite, however, has to trundle around under its own [battery] power, which means there's less available for suction. In his book *Why We Buy: The science of shopping*, retail anthropologist Paco Underhill notes that power is an important factor when it comes to choosing a vacuum cleaner:

> 'When we interviewed men shopping for vacuum cleaners and asked which feature was most important, their [predictable] answer: "Suck". Read: *Power*. Home appliances have gotten more macho as men have gotten less so.'

The Trilobite has 90 watts (although the dirt has just a few inches to travel); the average Dyson has 1,200, at a fraction of the cost. Recall the P3 model of Power, Performance and Perception and remember it's perception of power that counts, not the reality. Just looking at those figures, does the Trilobite seem to be up to the job?

RIGHT IDEA, WRONG CONTEXT?

Beyond the domestic jungle of dining room chairs and lethally-fringed rugs, technology like RoboVac is more likely to find a grateful home in environments such as factories or hospitals, where long, uncluttered corridors present fewer practical barriers to its use. Likewise, many of the innovative ideas dreamed up for the domestic kitchen are being applied in factories and industrial settings around the world. Monitoring the inner workings of a domestic microwave may sound like connectivity gone mad but using remote diagnostics to monitor the health of an expensive piece of industrial machinery is a no-brainer by anyone's standards. So too is the remote updating of software, especially when hundreds of machines need the latest version – in the typical office, for example.

The networked fridge may be an icon of 'technology for the sake of it', but the rationale for networking a vending machine and allowing it to reorder when it's running low is compelling. Still, the drip drip drip of technological progress may ensure that one day our appliances really do connect to the internet and reorder milk when we're short. And by that time, who knows, computers may be as reliable as the humble fridge.

NOTES

1 *mpulse*, 23 June 2001.
2 *Being Digital*, Hodder & Stoughton, 1995.

Innovation in the office

'It is a difficult business to impose new technologies on ingrained, incumbent work practices.'
Abigail Sellen and Richard Harper
The Myth of the Paperless Office

While innovation in the home is designed to make our lives easier and more pleasant by automating many of the humdrum tasks we perform from day to day, innovation in the office is designed to make us – and the economy – more productive.

No one doubts the huge benefits that computers and the internet have brought to the modern office. Journalists of today stand in awe of hacks who worked in the days of hot metal, typing paragraphs on to single sheets of paper (with typewriters!) then working the story with scissors and glue.

Information technology has made it easier for us to create documents, file them, search them and send them. Our accounting systems have been revolutionized to the extent that Cisco Systems chief executive John Chambers talks about his company closing its books within hours of the year's end. We can track sales leads, drill into customer databases, find patterns in sales figures and present them to the board using nothing more than a laptop computer – and all because of IT.

But getting innovation of any kind accepted in the workplace is a little more complicated than marketing to an audience of individual consumers. Take, for example, an idea to computerize expense claims in the office. For it to be successful, the new expenses system would have to be accepted by the accounts department, the wages department, the IT department, the IT manager, senior management, the head of purchasing and – most importantly – the people who would actually use it. The system may have to interface with several existing IT packages including accounts and payroll. It may create new procedures and new pathways of approval that have to be learned by different members of staff. All of these factors must be taken into account and all the relevant groups of staff must be brought on board – by mandate if necessary – in order for the new expenses system to succeed.

People are more likely to comply with a request when:
- a reason is provided
- there is give and take
- they see others complying
- the request comes from someone they respect or like
- the request comes from a legitimate source of authority.

Source: Robert B Cialdini. *Influence: Science and practice*, HarperCollins, 1993

Many innovative IT projects have failed because key users resisted – possibly because they didn't perceive any benefit to the new way of doing things, or because they resented change being imposed on them. What's more, the adoption of innovations within companies depends on how innovative they are (remember that companies themselves range from innovators to laggards), their economic situation and the cost of switching, which includes the time spent learning to use the new system.

Does IT really increase profitability?

Has information technology failed to deliver its promise of increased profits through greater efficiency? It sounds counter-intuitive, but one controversial researcher believes it has. Paul Strassmann argues that there is no relationship between the amount of money companies spend on IT and the profits they make. The author of books including *Information Productivity* and *The Squandered Computer*, Strassmann's credentials are impressive: he was in charge of defence information at the Department of Defence and was also chief information officer at companies including Kraft and Xerox.

Strassmann's views echo those of the Nobel Prize-winning economist Robert Solow, who in 1987 suggested that computers could be seen everywhere but the productivity statistics! Throughout his career, Strassmann has been collecting statistics on IT investment. He accepts that in the decade to 1999, US companies lowered the cost of the information management (IM) required to deliver goods and services. It takes less IM to manage assets than it did a decade ago. But analyzing thousands of companies, he finds no correlation between per employee IT investment and profitability. Instead, he argues, recent gains in productivity (and profits) have resulted from low interest rates and good management of the economy.

Strassmann notes that in 92% of major US corporations, the cost of IM exceeds the cost of capital ownership. IM costs include managing, co-ordinating, training, communicating, planning, accounting, marketing and research. In fact, just about everything that isn't a direct input into delivering a product or service to a customer. Information management also includes HR, financial expenses, purchasing, lobbying, regulatory compliance and costs associated with creating a relationship with customers and suppliers. He defines 'Information Productivity' as 'Economic Value Added' divided by 'Information Management Costs'.

While it would be ridiculous to suggest that companies shouldn't invest in IT, Strassman argues that the main reason companies do so is because they are involved in an ever-spiralling arms race with their competitors.

THE FUTURE OF THE OFFICE?

In spite of hurdles like these, conventional wisdom holds that IT innovations in the office will enable companies to streamline their business processes, improve efficiency and increase profits along the way. Businesses will save millions on paper costs alone, according to futurists who tell us (and have been telling us for the past 30 years) that the office will soon be a paperless environment. Email and videoconferencing will revolutionize business communications and democratize the hierarchical structure of the firm; office politics will be a thing of the past because, apparently, there will be no offices! Broadband internet and virtual telepresence will consign the daily commute to the scrapheap of history and 'always on, always every-where' wireless internet will enable us to work as productively from the beach as we do in the offices of today.

The longer-term future is even rosier, the visionaries believe. In March 2000, *Fortune* magazine asked four of America's largest office design companies to predict how the workplace will look in 2050. Not surprisingly their prognostications reflected the day's *zeitgeist* of constant connectivity and ubiquitous computing:

● chairs that float around the office through magnetic levitation, complete with wireless links that communicate with an implant in your head, so that all you have to do is think about information and it appears in holographic projection above your desk. (It didn't say what would appear if you thought about sex or soccer, which many of us are prone to do in the office!)
● holographic videoconferencing
● telepresence with holographic images of colleagues projected around the office
● phones and PCs will have disappeared into walls and into our clothes
● noise-cancelling technologies will silence the office din
● office dividers will have adjustable opacity for privacy at the flick of a switch.

Between now and 2050, however, it might be nice if some of the inno-vations already in the workplace would actually do what the visionaries promised! Far from heralding a new era of four-hour days and more leisure time than we have hobbies to fill, computers have increased the workload so that we now work longer hours than ever before. Email has been adopted with such enthusiasm that some offices are banning its use on Fridays because of information overload – a concept that many technologists still haven't grasped as they develop yet more innovative ways to overload us!

COMMUTING – A SENTENCE!

On the face of it, commuting has to be about the dumbest activity in history. Every week, millions of people waste time and money travelling to and from work, either in environmentally damaging cars or on trains that are often so crowded that even reading a newspaper is impossible; and yet we still do it.

In the UK, just 1.1% of all workers are true teleworkers, according to a report entitled *The Future of Work: Telework – The new industrial revolution,* produced by the Trades Union Congress (TUC) in 2001. Arguing that most teleworking in the UK is 'old wine in new bottles', the report identified three categories of teleworkers making up about 1.5 million or 5.7% of the UK workforce:

- **Teleworker home workers:** True teleworkers who do their main job from home (1.1% of all workers).
- **Home-based teleworkers:** People who work in different locations using their home as a base, for example, service engineers and agency staff. These make up 2.9% of the UK workforce.
- **Occasional teleworkers:** People who work from home at least one day a week (1.7%).

A more recent study published by the UK's Office of National Statistics in June 2002 suggested the figure was slightly higher, at 7%.

By comparison, nearly 17% of the workforce of Finland are teleworkers, while in Sweden more than 15% work from home. The TUC report observes:

'It is noticeable that the economies where telework is most common are those with wide access to the new technologies and with a strong framework of social and labour market protections.'

The arguments for teleworking are compelling:

- It saves the time, expense and stress of commuting, allowing staff to start work on time and in a better frame of mind.
- The company saves money on office space.
- Staff have more time for themselves and their families.
- 'Wardrobe costs' are reduced.
- Absenteeism is likely to be reduced, as are stress-related problems.
- Staff can work from places where housing is less expensive, leading to social changes.
- Staff have greater mobility and needn't find a new job if their partner has to move to a new location.
- Major cities will benefit from less traffic.

But however good a proposition it looks on paper, there are sound arguments against teleworking:

- The loss of social contact – working at home can be lonely.
- The loss of immediate support from colleagues.
- The lack of supervision and monitoring of staff performance and the potential for abuse.
- Problems with access to stored information, especially if it is paper-based.
- The home may not be a good environment in which to work.
- The inability to have spontaneous 'water cooler' meetings with colleagues.
- The loss of the political aspects of office life – ambitious staff may want to be at the centre of things, while those who telework may be regarded as unambitious.
- Staff must become much more self-sufficient with technology and sort out problems themselves instead of relying on technical support.
- The loss of a clearly-defined work-life boundary.

How many of these issues can be solved with better technology? Will broadband internet, videoconferencing, instant messaging and holographic telepresence really deal with the issue of loneliness or a feeling of isolation? Will technology address the needs for company, discipline, spontaneity, team spirit and motivation, or the feeling of being involved? It's unlikely. Maybe Finland is as good as it gets for teleworking.

A study carried out in the UK, entitled *Work-Life Balance 2000*,[1] found that only a third of all employees would rather work at home. That means the other two-thirds would rather put up with the time, expense and hassle of commuting. Obviously they don't perceive any advantage in working from home, however good the technology. In addition, nearly 90% of the workers interviewed felt that their bosses would rather they came to work every day, which suggests that companies value close supervision and immediate interaction above the cost savings they could generate.

Here's another interesting observation. Back in the dotcom boom, when dynamic young techno-enthusiastic entrepreneurs were claiming that the internet was going to change the world, were they:

a) Creating virtual companies and teleworking from home using all the latest internet technology to cut office costs and increase productivity?
b) Being dinosaurs like the rest of us and commuting to offices in dotcom hotspots like Clerkenwell in London or Silicon Alley in New York so they could interact with their colleagues and wallow in the buzz?

IS THE AGE OF THE VIDEOPHONE *FINALLY* HERE?

Along with magnetic levitation and the paperless office, videophones are one of futurology's most enduring flops, having failed to take off despite the repeated prognostications of so-called visionaries over the past 40 years. But like the man who shouts 'earthquake' every day in San Francisco, it seems likely that the forecasters will eventually be proved right; and at least this is one innovation that has a fighting chance with the arrival of broadband internet, the technologist's cure for everything bar hunger.

I was about to write something to the effect that the onward march of technological progress would inevitably drive corporate users towards videoconferencing – the office version of the videophone. But the tragic fact is that the lapses of a few airport security guards have done more to boost the videoconferencing industry than any improvement in bandwidth or video compression technology.

Before the atrocities of 11 September 2001, the technology already existed to hold meetings in a videoconferencing suite. But the vast majority of executives preferred to get on a plane and travel hundreds of miles for that look in the eye and the firm handshake because, however costly and inconvenient it was, the personal touch worked. Travelling somewhere to meet someone is a signal that you value them. What's more, those subtle nuances, the glances and the body language have been hard for video-conferencing systems to pick up. Although the latest crop project DVD-quality images on to 42 inch screens, it seems that the face-to-face business meeting is unlikely to face a serious challenge from video technology.

Does the internet create more travel, not less?

At the same time as techno-enthusiasts were forecasting the death of travel, thanks to the emergence of a global communications network, business travel from the UK actually grew by 33% in the five years to 2000, according to research published by the Association of British Travel Agents, in November 2001. One possible reason is that the internet helped to generate more sales leads that needed to be followed up in person.

Countries with the highest penetration of telecommunications also have the highest levels of mobility and if global communications are about to put the dampers on international travel, no one has bothered to tell the folks planning the new £5 billion terminal at Heathrow Airport. Likewise, London's planners are reckoning on more commuters in the future, not less. So much for teleworking and the idea that the internet will reduce the need to travel!

(At this point in the first draft I wrote the following aside: 'But can't you just bet that some technologist at MIT is beavering away on a system that replicates the firm handshake using force-feedback gloves linked to a wireless broadband internet link?' Lo and behold, the very next day, *Wired* magazine reported that such a system actually was in development at MIT Media Lab (where else?). What's more, its developer suggested that using a virtual handshake might be a good way for business executives to close on deals – which proves my earlier point about technologists always giving bad examples of what their inventions can do.)

After September 11, however, people have shown themselves slightly more willing to forego the handshake and the body language, but this change in attitude has absolutely nothing to do with improvements in videoconferencing technology.

If – or maybe when – it finally takes off, video telephony will throw up some interesting behavioural problems: how will we be able to read a newspaper or check email when we're on the videophone having a really boring conversation? What if we're undressed when the phone goes? Will callers feel offended if we put them on audio only?

HAVE YOUR AVATAR CALL MINE

Having failed to grasp the bit about why people prefer the personal touch (what have they got against human contact?), technologists are now working on the next innovation in business communications – avatars.

In their *2001 Technology Timeline*, the visionaries at BTexact Technologies forecast the emergence of avatar-based communications by 2002 (and the advent of the paperless office by 2005!). Like much technological futurology, however, the prediction was couched in astrologically vague terms.

Does 'Use of talking head technology for conferencing – 2002' mean it will exist in a laboratory or it will be adopted widely by business, or does it really mean that it will take off in the home and not in business? Remember from Chapter 5 that *Megamistakes* author Steven Schnaars complained that most technological forecasting was too vague to be evaluated properly.

If it's intended for business, avatar-based conferencing is based on the

Behavioural Premise that serious business executives will forego face-to-face meetings, videoconferencing, audio-conferencing, plain old phone calls and even Instant Messaging so that they can meet in cyberspace and be represented around a virtual table by something that looks like a character from *The Sims*!

Avatars may be great fun in sci-fi conventions and multiplayer online games (notice a somewhat nerdy pattern emerging here?) and one called Ananova even reads the news headlines on her own website. But surely doing business is a bit more serious than playing *EverQuest* or hanging out in the *Habbo Hotel*! Ask yourself how you'd like to interview a candidate for an important job in your organization: face to face, by video link, by phone or by avatar? If you couldn't do it face to face, would you use any of the alternatives or would you reschedule?

BTexact is also developing supposedly photorealistic looking avatars to advise people on mortgages and financial services over the internet. The technology met with derision from financial services companies when it was reported (by a business journalist) on BBC News in April 2002, but doubtless the boffins will press on regardless. After all, why should a lack of consumer enthusiasm stop innovation in its tracks – that's what R&D is all about!

THE RISE AND FALL OF HOT DESKING

Another office innovation that has yet to catch on is hot desking – the idea that nobody 'owns' their own workspace in the office, so anyone can sit anywhere they like and access their computer files from any terminal. Hot desking was most famously tried at the offices of Chiat/Day, the advertising agency, in New York and Venice, California, and documented in the pages of *Wired* magazine in February 1999.

Back in 1993, agency founder Jay Chiat wanted to create a virtual office by removing all the usual workspaces and personal cubicles and equipping his staff with cellular phones and laptop computers that could be used anywhere in the building. It was an audacious move that was hailed as signalling the end of the conventional workplace and all of its petty hierarchical constraints. Instead of corner offices and wooden dividers there were open-plan working areas with couches and coffee tables where colleagues who wouldn't normally meet each other in the office could have spontaneous and supposedly creative interaction.

Unfortunately, Chiat's dream turned out to be a nightmare for staff, who queued every morning for a laptop and a phone, then raced around the office trying to find a place to work. The loss of an organized office geography meant people wasted even more time hunting down colleagues and, in the end, people began using their cars as filing cabinets so they could put their hands on everything they needed for work. Their misery was made worse by the fact that Chiat would roam around the office demanding to know why people were occupying the same space as they had done the previous day. Chiat sold out in 1995 and, soon after, the new owners, Omnicom, declared his bold experiment dead.

Apart from the drive of a headstrong, ego-involved innovator who imposed his own vision of the world on his staff without first testing the market, could the failure of hot desking at Chiat/Day have been foretold with a little critical thinking? The answer is probably, yes.

Surprisingly, most of us have a lot of experience of hot desking – at school! We spent our days moving from subject to subject, from class to class, but here's the clue: we probably sat in the same seat for every lesson. Now, as adults, we go to conferences and awayday meetings and, after the coffee breaks, more often than not we return to the same seat we were sitting in before, even if we haven't bagged it with a conference brochure or a briefcase. The same phenomenon happens every Sunday morning in churches up and down the country!

What this illustrates is obvious – we are both territorial and creatures of habit. We like our own personal space in the office because it gives us a sense of comfort and reassurance and the feeling of being part of a team. That's why we decorate our dividers and clutter our desks with paper in our idiosyncratic little ways. The office can be stressful enough as it is; why make it worse by forcing us into unfamiliar surroundings every day and removing what little comfort we already have?

Emotional issues aside, hot desking requires technological changes as well. Chiat/Day's philosophy of checking phones and laptops out and back in every day sounds inefficient by today's standards, when laptops can log in wirelessly and phone systems can follow people from desk to desk, but systems like these cost money. Where Chiat/Day failed, however, many other companies are making a form of hot desking work, but by and large they are the ones with nomadic staff who come and go and work from home as well. A few advertising agencies still espouse hot desking for its funky, spontaneous 'we're so different' image – but then they would, wouldn't they? For the rest of us, hot desking fails that simple test of any innovation: is it better than what we already do? The answer, it seems, is no.

WHY GROUPWARE FAILS IN THE OFFICE

Office software comes in two varieties: packages such as spreadsheets and word processors that support individual users, and 'groupware' which is designed to support the collaborative activities of groups. The expenses system mentioned at the beginning of the chapter is one example of groupware; calendar systems are another – they enable meeting organizers to check the diaries of members of staff so that a convenient meeting time can be scheduled for everyone.

One of the leading authorities on the use of groupware in companies is Jonathan Grudin, formerly of the University of California in Irvine and now a researcher at Microsoft. Arguing that failures in groupware implementation come not from technical problems but from failing to understand the social dynamics of how people actually use groupware, Grudin identifies eight challenges facing developers[2]:

- **Critical mass:** Groupware only works if everyone uses it. Calendaring systems, for example, are no use if people don't play the game and keep their diaries up to date so that everyone else can see what they're up to.
- **There is a disparity between the effort and benefit of using the software:** While everyone needs to use groupware for it to succeed, the fact is that some people will gain no perceivable benefit from doing so. Why should someone use a collective calendaring system if they don't need to schedule meetings with it?
- **There is a disruption of social processes:** Groupware can force people into behaviours that don't fit with the real world. Can anyone schedule

the boss into a meeting or does his or her assistant do that? What's more, just because the boss's time isn't booked up in the calendar, it doesn't mean it's free. Another example might be a plan for all journalists on a newspaper to pool their address books into a central database for the benefit of everyone. Hacks are very protective of their contacts and they'd almost certainly resist.

- **There are problems handling unusual situations:** Can developers second-guess every situation that might arise, or do users have to fit in with the way the developers think? Standardizing procedures for the benefit of a computer may be counter-productive.

- **Groupware features may not be used very often:** Grudin cites the example of a co-authorship package developed specifically to let writers collaborate on documents. The problem is that the writers themselves may spend more time working alone using a single-user word processor. Why give up that familiarity to use a co-authorship package once in a while? Likewise, why use a group calendar for those occasional meetings if you already use Palm Desktop software every day?

- **How do you design for a group and evaluate the use of group-ware?** User interface specialists tend to watch individuals using software for only a few hours. Groupware involves social dynamics and pro-cedures that may span days, even weeks. Think about the expenses system – the approvals process may take a couple of weeks and involve several people. How do you study that, or do you just impose your own ideas of how things should work and expect users to fall in with it?

- **Informal processes can be lost, along with intuitive thinking:** Decision-support groupware can remove the spontaneous and informal aspects of decision-making if it imposes rigid structures on the way things are done. What's more, the decision to implement groupware may come from a biased party, for example an IT director who hasn't stopped to consider the importance of these informal business processes.

- **How do you recruit everyone who needs to be on board?** As Grudin points out, a word processor liked by just 20% of the potential market can still be a big success. Groupware that is liked by just 20% of the people supposed to be using it will definitely fail – and at a cost.

YOU HAVE [TOO MUCH] MAIL

Email is one of those hugely successful innovations that hasn't quite worked as planned. What we were promised was a revolutionary new communications system that would cut costs, boost productivity and democratize the workplace. But, like the computer before it, email has only added to the daily workload as we wade through hundreds of messages a week – most of which add very little value or insight to our working lives. Far from replacing face-to-face meetings or phone calls, it seems email creates more need for human contact, while the much-hyped technology for democratizing the office has in reality become the favourite tool of office politics. If that wasn't bad enough, email has now become a gateway for junk marketing spam and virus attacks that cost billions to deal with.

Email overload has reached such proportions that in the UK, companies such as Thomson, Rowntree and the National Lottery operator Camelot have introduced email free Fridays to give their staff a break from the constant demands that this innovative technology has imposed on them. Yet the computer and communications industries are sailing full steam ahead to develop wireless internet devices that will overload us even more. Soon, there will be no escape from the demands of a technology that was supposed to make our lives easier and more productive! Don't knock it, say the technologists – that's progress! Of course, there is an argument that wireless email could help people manage their email when they have 'down time' out of the office, perhaps when going to a meeting by taxi or when waiting to go into a meeting. But if other devices such as mobile phones are anything to go by, the impression that someone is permanently contactable will probably lead to an overall increase in the amount of messages they receive.

Dr Steve Brown, a psychologist at Loughborough University in the UK, has studied the use of email in corporate settings and describes it as a 'double-edged sword'. He says: 'On the one hand you can't do without it and it would be silly for a company not to use it, but the fact is it does a lot of things its designers never intended. People thought email would speed up communication within companies and democratize the structure so that anyone could email the CEO, but that hasn't happened.' Instead, he observes, managers spend much of their time in drawn out and unwieldy exchanges that ultimately require a face-to-face meeting to resolve. What's more, the further executives climb up the corporate ladder, the more insulated they become from their email – they have someone else who deals with it!

COPY THAT

Ignoring spam – which can usually be filtered or deleted without reading – the real productivity killer is the 'cc' or carbon copy function, which enables staff to send the same message to any number of colleagues. 'People are concerned about the sheer amount of time they spend in front of their screens, constantly having to keep up with email,' Dr Brown explains. 'There's a feeling that even if you don't need to reply, you have to read every message just to keep track of what's going on, otherwise you'll be left behind.' People refer to this as 'loopmail' because they have to read it just to stay in the loop.

The 'cc' function creates problems in two ways: firstly, people copy colleagues and managers into conversations that are of little relevance to them. If replies are also copied back to all recipients instead of just the sender, the number of messages can quickly spiral out of control. Apart from the drain on people's time – remember they may be monitoring the messages just for the sake of keeping up – the conversation can become unwieldy and confusing, especially because people insist on including the original message in their reply. Imagine ten people adding their two cents worth to every message they receive and then copying back to the group – it will soon become hard to follow what's going on. Dr Brown says: 'It's difficult to see who said what when you have to scroll down a long message, especially if people add notes or edit earlier threads. Where you expect a linear sequence you don't get one and so you have to read multiple copies of a message that is slightly different each time.' This can cause problems when trying to create a definitive 'history' of what was actually written down, because several versions exist. The end result is confusion that frequently has to be sorted out in face-to-face meetings. Bear in mind also that the messages have to be stored somewhere – at a cost to the bottom line.

The second problem of copying in is that it can be used as a political tool. By emailing someone to ask where the sales figures are, and copying it to several other members of staff, a manager can place pressure on the addressee and all the other recipients. In addition, notes Dr Brown, people frequently store emails for later use as political leverage. 'It's like gathering an audience in an arena,' he observes. 'There's a lot of ass-covering and how it works is that someone will put out an innocuous message like "I see the sales figures are down; I wonder why that might be?" and of course everyone goes into ass-covering mode and starts replying because they feel they have to.' Thinking up a good reply takes time, which is bad for productivity.

In the days before most of us had email, the effort of writing and distributing paper memos was a barrier to the kinds of behaviours we see today in the use of email as a political tool and the liberal use of the 'cc' function. But rather than educating workers to send less email and use their social skills a bit more, visionaries want us to put our faith in another of technology's great panaceas – intelligent software agents that promise to filter out all the noise and leave us to concentrate on the signal. One of the joys of working in technology is that you can make a nice living by creating innovative new technologies to sort out all the unforeseen problems created by innovative old technologies. It remains to be seen whether intelligent agents will create unforeseen problems of their own, but if the history of office technology is anything to go by, the chances are they will.

WHY PAPER IS HERE TO STAY

It seems incredible, but after 30 years of getting it hopelessly wrong, visionary futurists are still holding out for the advent of the paperless office instead of focusing their attention on why attempts to implement it have so far failed. Luckily, a couple of cognitive scientists who study how technology is actually used by real people in the real world have produced an excellent book called *The Myth of the Paperless Office*, which ought to be compulsory reading for anyone even remotely involved in the development of new technology.

Ask a technologist why paper is still around and they will probably talk about screen resolution, portability, viewing angle, contrast and lighting (and I'm sure broadband will doubtless creep in there as well!). But according to authors Abigail Sellen and Richard Harper, the persistence of paper so far – and into the future – has little to do with the inadequacies of today's or tomorrow's technology. Until developers understand this, they will continue to produce expensive technological solutions that are doomed to fail.

The concept of the paperless office first came to prominence in the early 1970s when emerging computer technologies promised new ways to process information. Thanks to some technological hype and a fair dollop of gee-whizz journalism, what Sellen and Harper call the 'myth' of the paperless office took off. The paperless office quickly became the poster child of technology's brighter future and the desire of companies to go paperless was more often than not a desire to throw out a visible symbol of old thinking and appear progressive.

As we now know, paper consumption has actually increased since the 1970s because computers and the World Wide Web have created more documents for us to read and, more importantly, *use*. If all we wanted to do was read a document, we could do that on a computer screen; but paper allows us to do so much more than just read. What we do with the printout is as much a part of the process as actually reading it.

Consider two Post-It Notes that contain pretty much the same amount of information: one says 'Ring Bob' and the other says 'Ring Mary'. Imagine you return to your desk after lunch and 'Ring Bob' has been placed on the desk next to your keyboard, while 'Ring Mary' is stuck *on* the keyboard. Do the two notes still convey similar amounts of information, or does 'Ring Mary', through its physical location, convey a greater sense of urgency? Of course, the person leaving the messages could fire up the Stickies program on your PC and write both messages in different type styles, but somehow I think that if there was a scrap of paper nearby they'd reach for a pen instead.

This physical, tangible nature of paper has both benefits and drawbacks that affect its use in the office.

THE ADVANTAGES OF PAPER

- It can be grasped, carried, manipulated, folded and marked, as can anything made from it, such as a book.
- It is good for immediate tasks such as writing notes.
- It can be laid out, shared and annotated during collaborative work.
- It can signal its importance, for example the 'Ring Mary' Post-It Note. Another example might be in a meeting where people are looking at two documents; everyone can see who is taking notice of which pieces of paper and how much attention each document is receiving. Try doing that with laptops!
- It has symbolic importance – handing over a completed report is a symbolic act, more formal than simply emailing someone a PDF file.
- Printouts of documents allow us to 'clutter' our desks in a way that makes sense to us; for example, we place paper according to when we will need it next. This means we can work with several documents in view, which is hard to do on a computer, even with a large screen.
- It allows authoring, reviewing, planning and collaboration. We can annotate it without changing the original document.

THE DISADVANTAGES OF PAPER

- It allows local use only.
- Its distribution is costly.
- It cannot be modified (as opposed to annotated).
- Filing it is expensive.
- Filed documents cannot be searched easily.

What electronic systems do much better than paper are file, search and distribute information, which is why the ambition of a paperless office is not at all misguided. It's just that when it comes to using the information, paper is much more versatile than a computer screen.

WHY DO WE READ?

Sellen and Harper argue that by focusing on technical issues such as screen resolution, viewing angle and contrast, companies developing paperless technologies have ignored the central questions of how and why we read documents in the office:

> 'Those who design and develop technologies of reading have often been more interested in getting the best performance from their hardware and software than in properly understanding what reading involves.'

Experiments studying reading speed, scanning and the clarity of screens have therefore missed the point. Instead, the authors argue, developers need to understand what the process of reading actually involves and what other processes it supports. There are many reasons we need to read documents in the office: as part of filling in forms; to absorb information; to cross-reference; to summarize and make notes; to identify things; to skim; to search; to learn; to review; to support listening and discussion.

In a study of 15 people, ranging from an airline pilot to an optician, Sellen and Harper made the following observations:

- 82% of their activities involved the use of documents.
- Paper-based reading accounted for 85% of all reading.
- Reading frequently involved several documents, either on paper or on screen.
- Reading usually supported writing.

In addition, they observed that people navigate and read documents using both hands and that one hand could turn a page and hold a pen at the same time. On a computer, navigation requires a certain amount of point and click precision and a hand operating a track pad or a mouse cannot easily hold a pen to make notes.

In conclusion, Sellen and Harper argue that paper is better for reading in the office because:

- **It is tangible:** We can easily flick through it, skim it, jump backwards and forwards and use both hands to do all of this and annotate as well.
- **It is flexible in time and space:** This allows us to lay it out however

we need – the most important papers on top, lesser documents on the periphery. All of us clutter our desks with paper in a remarkably logical and meaningful way. Imagine having five windows open on a computer screen and keeping unopened documents somewhere handy for use on the hard drive.

● **It is tailorable:** Meaning that we can annotate it without changing it, by adding an extra layer of text on to the original. On a computer this is a more complicated operation involving the use of editing menus.

● **It is easily manipulated:** We can push documents around to suit our immediate needs.

Looking at these advantages, not one has anything to do with resolution, viewing angle or ease of reading. Replicating the feel of paper with a flexible high resolution and an infinitely programmable screen may be a great solution to an entirely different set of problems from those we encounter when reading in the office! Will one device like this suit our needs when we have to look at three different documents at the same time? Why buy three paper-like screens when you can simply print out three documents on paper and lay them out so that you can refer to them all at the same time?

Rather than hoping to achieve a paperless office, Sellen and Harper suggest that companies combine the strengths of both paper and electronic media: paper for its tangibility and immediacy and electronic systems for their storage capacity, ease of searching and distribution. Whatever the technological visionaries say, it looks like this glorious ancient technology will be around for a long time to come.

NOTES

1 *Work-Life Balance 2000: A baseline study of work-life balance practices in Great Britain.* Terence Hogarth.

2 *Groupware and Social Dynamics: Eight challenges for developers.* In RM Baecker, J Grudin, WAS Buxton and S Greenberg (Eds.), *Readings in Human-Computer Interaction: Toward the year 2000.*

The best laid plans of men with mice

'There is no reason for any individual to have a computer in the home.'

Ken Olsen
Chairman, Digital Equipment Corporation, 1977

As Ken Olsen's famous comment shows, forecasts about the future of computing almost inevitably tend towards the conservative, as innovators find wonderful new things to do with them. No one doubts that computers and communications devices will play an increasingly important role in our lives as we move towards what technologists refer to as 'pervasive computing'. What the visionaries foresee is something like a scene from the Steven Spielberg film *Minority Report* – a world in which everything is connected to everything else and information is on tap wherever we need it. Sensors in our homes will monitor our every movement, adjusting heating and lighting as we move around the house, while flat screens on every wall will alternate between displaying works of art, stock prices and our diary for the day. Our bodies will be monitored by computers embedded in our clothes, which will relay their information over the wireless internet so that our fridge can customize a dietary programme and order the appropriate food from the online grocery store.

We'll walk down the street aided by location-sensitive augmented visual reality, complete with avatars floating in front of our eyes to tempt us into nearby shops with specially personalized offers that our intelligent agents just *know* we want to buy.

When we travel to work, our vehicles will select their own routes based on dynamic road pricing and traffic monitoring and we'll sit back as the car joins a computer-controlled convoy and drives itself to the office. (This future commuting scenario assumes we aren't teleworking by broadband virtual holo-tele-presence – you know, the one that includes the tactile glove so we can still enjoy the firm handshake!)

Of course, whether any of these utopian innovations are actually wanted, needed, practical, technically possible or economically viable is another matter, and one that rarely seems to bother the wide-eyed futurists who trot out such Panglossian visions for the benefit of an unquestioning media.

What *is* clear, however, is that as computers become more complex and begin to blend into the background of everyday life, our relationship with them may have to evolve, forcing us to interact with them in ways more imaginative than today's keyboard, mouse and screen. Virtual reality, speech recognition, virtual keyboards, computers that emit smells, cursors driven by eye and head movements, retinal projectors, intelligent agents and computers that talk have been in the works for a while now. But how they challenge the incumbent interface of screen and keyboard remains to be seen. Familiar ways of working are often more resilient than innovators would like.

WAS DVORAK REALLY BETTER THAN QWERTY?

The familiar Qwerty keyboard we use on computers today is one of technology's most resilient standards. It was patented in 1878 and has survived the progression from primitive mechanical typewriter to today's laptop computers, seeing off early attempts at voice and pen-driven computing along the way. But the Qwerty design has also seen off rival keyboard layouts that claimed to make typing faster and more efficient.

History's biggest challenge to the Qwerty keyboard came in the 1930s when August Dvorak invented the Dvorak Keyboard, claiming it would revolutionize the typing pool by making typists far more productive. The story of the Dvorak Keyboard is usually portrayed as an example of an innovative and superior technology that failed because consumers made the wrong choice, just as the supposedly inferior VHS trounced Betamax in the early days of home video recorders. But was it really better?

According to professors Stan Liebowitz of the University of Texas and Stephen Margolis of North Carolina State University, the accepted version of the Dvorak story is wrong. In a controversial paper published in the *Journal of Law and Economics*, back in April 1990, they argue that the Dvorak Keyboard offered little or no relative advantage to the Qwerty design and so there was little incentive to switch. The paper is also summarized in the June 1996 edition of *Reason* magazine in which they write: 'The story of the Dvorak's superiority is a myth or, more properly, a hoax.'

The Qwerty keyboard was designed to stop typewriter keys jamming as one fell back and the next flicked upwards to strike the ribbon. It achieved this by separating popular combinations of letters so their mechanisms didn't become entangled. The Dvorak Keyboard, by contrast, was designed to reduce the effort of typing by putting the more commonly used keys under the strongest fingers and in a layout that minimized the distance the fingers had to travel to strike them in the course of a typical document. Nowadays, with no mechanical typewriters, computers can easily be reconfigured to operate with the Dvorak layout instead of Qwerty. On Apple's G4 laptops, for example, it's simply a case of telling the computer to use Dvorak and rearranging the keys in the right places.

So if the layout is so much better, why don't we use it? According to Liebowitz and Margolis, the reason we haven't all switched is because the Dvorak Keyboard simply isn't better. Although supporters of the Dvorak Keyboard claim that studies have shown it allows faster typing speeds and quicker learning times than Qwerty, the authors argue that these studies were tainted by the lack of adequate controls, poor comparisons and the fact that Dvorak himself was involved in an influential study conducted by the US Navy.

The authors also claim that later studies carried out by America's General Services Administration appear to refute the notion that it was a more effective layout to use. Typing speeds on Dvorak could match but rarely exceed those on Qwerty keyboards, and, with additional training, typists who were already using Qwerty could improve their speeds to well beyond those achievable on Dvorak. In addition, they cite research conducted at IBM, which also found no significant advantage for the Dvorak layout over the incumbent design of Qwerty.

Whatever the objective truth,[1] checking it against the characteristics of innovations from Chapter 3 shows that the Dvorak Keyboard is 'trialable' on any decent computer where the keys can be moved around. It has been tested and its results are 'observable' and, it seems, there is still debate as to whether it has any 'relative advantage' over the Qwerty design. It requires new learning because its layout is not 'compatible' with the way we are taught to type and some people may find its layout adds 'complexity' compared with what they already use.

In conclusion, Liebowitz and Margolis suggest that the Dvorak Keyboard was neither technically superior to the Qwerty layout, nor was it a better proposition overall. According to their arguments, the time and effort of retraining to use the Dvorak Keyboard would yield few, if any, benefits, so why bother switching? The fact that the debate rumbles on shows that sometimes it is difficult to assess whether an innovation really is innovative. What is certain, however, is that typists are voting with their fingers, which is why we still use Qwerty.

THE CUECAT: $180 MILLION LOST IN A SWIPE

Another innovation more recently seen off by the keyboard was the CueCat personal bar code scanner, designed to take the drudge out of typing internet addresses so that people could more easily find information on the net.

The brainchild of a charismatic entrepreneur, J Jovan Philyaw, and his Dallas-based company Digital:Convergence, the concept was simple: encourage advertisers to include bar codes on printed advertisements and develop a device to swipe the codes into a computer and take interested readers directly to the product's website. Advertisers would benefit from being able to track the impact of each advertisement and, with any luck, because finding the website would be made easier, more potential buyers would visit the site. In addition, people would be able to scan bar codes on product packaging to learn more about the product itself.

Of course, things didn't quite go as Philyaw planned and the CueCat has become something of an icon of failure in the history of dotcom madness. Through 1999 and 2000, Philyaw's almost evangelical fund-raising efforts netted more than $180 million in cash from some very smart companies including RadioShack, Coca-Cola, NBC and Belo Corp, which publishes newspapers including *The Dallas Morning News*. His plan was to distribute ten million of the feline devices through RadioShack and magazines such as *AdWeek*, *Forbes* and *Wired*. Each CueCat was reputed to have cost around $5 to manufacture!

According to a press release issued in August 2000, Philyaw said that market research had shown Digital:Convergence that 'consumers ... want a way to instantly link from stories they read ... to corresponding information on the internet.' The technology, he continued, 'will enable consumers to access unwieldy deep web content that, until now, has been difficult to access.'

Almost immediately after its launch, the CueCat met with derision from reviewers. MSN's *Slate* magazine referred to it as a 'stupid little geegaw', while gadget guru David Coursey of ZDNN, hit on the CueCat's underlying Behavioural Premise when he wrote: 'There is this crazy notion that people reading a print publication will dash to their computers to swipe a bar code for more information.'

Coursey's simple take on the technology proves that, sometimes, little questions are often the most penetrating – and the most overlooked by innovators. Despite the massive give-away, the CueCat flopped because people simply couldn't be bothered to use it. The CueCat's prospects weren't helped by the fact that many users raised concerns about privacy, which in turn generated a lot of negative press comment in the weeks after its launch.

In many cases, as Coursey predicted, CueCat owners were sitting nowhere near the computer when they were reading the advertisement and obviously couldn't be bothered to take the page over and scan it. The fact that an outsider could so easily spot such an obvious flaw in the plan emphasizes the fact that ego involvement and clear thinking don't mix in innovation.

For those who *were* interested in finding out more, using the CueCat obviously offered little 'relative advantage' over simply typing in the web address which, had the advertiser been smart, would have been as short as possible (for example, www.abc-company.com/offer), rather than the 'unwieldy, deep content' that Philyaw described. Perhaps people's perception was that plugging the CueCat into the back of the computer and installing its driver software was simply too much bother (even though it was a minor task) compared with the benefits it would bring.

Although bar code scanners have revolutionized stock control in stores, Digital:Convergence obviously misjudged how useful ordinary shoppers would find them. What's more, it seems they overestimated people's desire for more information – a failing that seems to be typical of technologists and one that has doomed many an otherwise innovative start-up over the past few years. In the CueCat's case, the end came just nine months after its launch, with four million devices left, mostly unused, in homes across America and a further six million languishing in warehouses.

Could this $180 million disaster have been avoided? In today's more sober funding environment the CueCat probably wouldn't get beyond the doorway of the average venture capitalist. But in the heady, optimistic and go-go days of the dotcom boom, when critical analysis was well and truly switched off, the world looked a whole lot different. The CueCat proposition obviously made very good sense to some very smart people, given the information they had and the environment in which they were making decisions.

But the fact is that the CueCat would have been simple to test among consumers before it was launched at such great expense – just give it to them and see whether they actually use it. If ever there was a case for behavioural and observational research being obligatory for innovative new gadgets, this was it (assuming, of course, that anyone would have taken notice of the research!). By spending a few thousand dollars and a couple of weeks studying what people did with the device in the real world, investors would have been better equipped to understand whether it was a winner or a loser.

PAPER ENTERS THE DIGITAL AGE

It's ironic that while many technologists have been predicting the end of paper and a new age of reading from computer screens that flex like paper, or from retinal displays that project information directly into our eyes, others are hatching plans for paper to challenge the screen and keyboard as the way we interact with computers. Companies such as Anoto, of Sweden, and OTM Technology, based in Israel, have been developing innovative new ways to input information using pen and paper – albeit more high-tech versions of this venerable double act.

Pen and paper are the simplest and yet probably the most important information technologies ever invented. They changed the course of human history by providing humanity with an external medium on which to store its knowledge, thus expanding the human intellect well beyond the limits of a single brain. By committing their thoughts to paper or other simple media like clay tablets, our ancestors were able to develop mathematics, art, science, commerce, religion and education – all of which dramatically increased the pace of human development. It's unlikely that any innovation will ever have as significant an impact as the simple combination of pen and paper and the development of writing.

Rather than reject this ancient technology as outdated and obsolete, Anoto, and its rivals have embraced it and brought it into the digital age. Christer Fåhraeus, Anoto's chief executive, says: 'The pen is the most common information technology in the world. There are billions of people using it and they learn how to use it from a very early age.' The problem with the pen, he argues, is that it is not 'connected'. What Anoto and its rivals have developed are wireless pens that write conventionally on paper but also transmit what they are writing to a nearby computer, PDA or mobile phone using Bluetooth or similar wireless technology. In this way, they hope to challenge the existing ways of recording information, turning handwriting into digits so it can be stored, used and distributed. For such innovative ideas to succeed, they will have to convince potential users that wireless pens offer a better proposition than pen and paper alone, keyboards or the kind of stylus-driven input common to most pocket computers like iPaqs or Palms. Anoto has produced a document comparing its technology with several alternatives – including the possibility of pens equipped with ultra-sensitive Global Positioning Systems – but *not* with ordinary pen and paper, which may turn out to be the Anoto system's biggest rival!

Of course, the proposition depends on the context. Very few people would write a long document using pen and paper when they could use a word processor instead (although the act of writing demands a more considered approach when committing words to paper, because editing them is so much more time consuming). By contrast, many people find it fiddly to type – or rather thumb – a text message on the small alphanumeric keyboard of a mobile phone, so the ability to write one with a wireless pen and beam it to the phone for onward dispatch may offer some 'relative advantage'.

DESIGNED FOR SUCCESS OR DOOMED TO FAIL?

Anoto is targeting several markets including that of the personal planner – so that people can write appointments into paper diaries and then beam them directly to a computer-based organizer. Its technology differs from OTM and other rivals because it knows exactly on what it's writing, be it a page in a diary or a tick box on a printed advertisement. The reason is that Anoto uses a specially developed paper, printed with an almost invisible pattern of dots that are detected by a small camera close to the nib of the pen. Anoto has developed a pattern so large – they claim it would cover half of the US if printed out – that small and unique regions of it could be licensed to different partners and used for specific purposes. In a diary, for example, the pattern for 9am on 1 January would be slightly different from the pattern for 1pm or 5pm. By writing an appointment in ink at a particular time and then transmitting it to a nearby PC, the pattern of dots recorded by the pen as it moved would be decoded by software in the PC and the appointment recorded in the right time slot. Other applications for Anoto include wireless email written on paper and sent by mobile phone or through a PC – imagine a memo pad with a large area for the message and then tick boxes saying SMS, Fax or Email. Likewise, a print advertisement could contain two tick boxes, one for 'Send me more information', the other for 'I would like to buy one'. Since every Anoto pen will have a unique code, back-end commerce servers at Anoto will identify the pen and its owner, the product it is buying and execute the transaction – for a small fee, of course. In some respects, the Anoto system is rather like the CueCat bar code scanner: both companies set out to make money by linking printed information to websites and electronic commerce using hand held technologies.

Another use for Anoto might be to automate crossword competitions in newspapers, since the solutions could be emailed to the judges as soon as they were complete and a computer could check that the answers were correct. In addition, many official bodies could deploy a system like Anoto to automate form-filling – assuming they weren't using keyboard entry to do the job.

Anoto is a truly innovative technology, but for it to succeed a lot of things have to happen:

- Anoto must convince pen manufacturers to license its technology and make Anoto pens.
- It must also convince paper companies to create useful paper products (diaries, memo pads etc) that are widespread enough for people to buy them easily (because Anoto won't work with ordinary scraps of paper).
- Advertisers must use the system so that Anoto can generate e-commerce revenues on top of licensing fees. How many times do people actually order goods from print advertisements and will Anoto make them more likely to order this way in the future?
- Pen manufacturers, paper printers and advertisers must feel there is sufficient commitment from each other to become involved. What's more, they must be convinced that a critical mass of users will buy in to the technology to make it worth their while. On a practical level, Anoto must have sufficient funding to see it through to the time when its product reaches critical mass.
- Wireless technology such as Bluetooth has to take off, or alternative ways to connect the pen will have to be developed.
- Anyone buying an Anoto pen must also have a wireless-enabled PC, phone or digital organizer capable of receiving the information from the pen, or they must upgrade (and consider it worth the extra expense).

- People must actually use the pen, so it has to be designed in a form that's familiar and convenient to them. Some people like fat pens, others prefer slimmer models. Weight, shape, battery life and the amount of ink it can hold are all important factors.
- Users must carry Anoto paper around with them if they want to use the pen. In the case of SMS, for example, is carrying a pen and paper as well as a phone really more convenient than just carrying the phone and using its keyboard to send a message?
- People must also be comfortable with the way the information is transferred and displayed on other devices, such as PC screens. Text is recorded graphically and needs further processing to turn it into characters that a computer can use – does this cause delays or other problems or does it require any new behaviours or inputs from the user?

Above all, people must actually believe that all of this technology offers them a better overall proposition than plain old pen and paper or its electronic alternatives such as other wireless pens, keyboards, styli or even voice-driven systems. For example, if a single tick can take the effort out of ordering an item in a catalogue by removing the need to fill in lots of personal details, then the 'relative advantage' may be considerable – depending, of course, on how often people order in this way. But if you write someone's phone number on a scrap of paper or put an appointment in your diary, is it really such a bother to type it into your PC or PDA? Don't forget that in the case of the CueCat, people decided that typing in a web address was less bother than scanning a bar code!

The *co-dependence* of Anoto's pen and its specially printed paper may prove to be its weakness compared with rivals such as OTM Technology's V-Pen, which can use any paper to hand (or any other reasonably firm surface). Like Anoto, OTM is licensing its core technology, which uses lasers to detect movement across the writing surface. OTM's chief executive, Gilad Lederer, is confident that pens, along with speech, will become the standard ways to interact with a computer. He says: 'What we feel people need is not just handwriting input but a replacement for the keyboard and mouse that's totally portable and which combines the navigational control of the mouse with the ability to enter text.'

WHY DO WE WRITE?

Perhaps the most fundamental issue facing wireless pen technologies such as Anoto and its rivals is this: why do we write? Just as the authors of *The Myth of the Paperless Office* studied why people read in the course of a typical day, it's important to understand what people are really doing when they put pen to paper. It might be to annotate and mark up documents, to fill in forms, to make appointments, to write messages, or to make notes that support typing or learning.

In cases like these, does the information really need to be transferred to a computer? For Anoto and its rivals, this is an important point. Think what happens when you go to a conference and take notes; do you type them up immediately when you return to your office or do you regard them merely as an *aide mémoire* – something you wrote to focus your attention on what was being said at the time? Think of how many occasions you might have to use a wireless pen throughout the day and ask yourself whether buying one would make sense, or whether it might actually create new uses for itself?

Of course, to suggest that wireless pens might fail because most of us are happy with computer keyboards or plain old pen and paper is to take a distinctly Western view of the world. More than two billion people don't use Roman alphabets that fit neatly on to a Qwerty keyboard, and wireless pens may have a great future in markets where people want to input text into a computer without the constraints imposed by Western keyboards.

TALKING SENSE?

Like broadband internet and faster processors, speech recognition seems to be one of technology's great cure-alls: as soon as we can talk to computers, technologists assure us, everything will be all right. Speech recognition technology is already finding useful commercial applications (for example filtering callers in call centres), while dictation software is making some inroads into specialist markets such as medicine and the law, where dictating machines are still a feature of working life.

But for voice commands to become a ubiquitous way of controlling a diverse array of computers and other machines, users will have to be convinced that talking really does make sense. For example, do we really need voice-activated light switches or TV remote controls when we can simply push a button? Do we really need to say 'dial home' when our phones have excellent speed dialling short cuts? What 'relative advantage' would such applications have over tried and trusted technologies as simple as the humble switch or a decent interface?

Given the increasing ease with which most of us can use computers and keyboards – where navigation has been simplified to clicking a menu or an icon, or pressing a set of short cut keys to get the job done – why bother talking? The point is that many people would rather interact quietly with a computer and not have to utter an endless stream of verbal commands such as 'file open' or 'file save', let alone dictate long passages or even hold a conversation. Even people working alone, who wouldn't be disturbing anyone else, may actually prefer to work in silence[2] and it has nothing to do with the quality of the technology itself. Even if dictation software were 100% accurate, 100% of the time, would we use it? What about voice fatigue, privacy, ease of working, and feeling self-conscious?

In his seminal book *The Invisible Computer*, cognitive scientist Don Norman points out that there is a big difference between recognizing words and understanding language. The advantage of keyboards, he argues, is that they allow precise and unambiguous input of words and commands. Furthermore, even if computers could understand language as well as humans, they would still face the same challenge of understanding what people actually *mean* rather than what they say.

Another problem is that people can be incredibly ungrammatical when they speak (try recording someone and transcribing what they say word for word!). Luckily the human brain is adept at ignoring the 'ums' and 'ahs' and 'ers' and our amazing ability to answer every question with the word 'well ...'. It can make sense of unfinished sentences or sentences without verbs or subjects, it can insert meaning where meaning is implied, it understands the tone and rhythm of speech and it can decode those subtle nuances of communication that are expressed not through words but through gesture and expression.

A more difficult challenge for speech recognition is what is going on inside our brains when we speak. Professor Ben Shneiderman, of the University of Maryland, has studied the problem and found that speaking and listening use the same part of the brain as short-term and working memory. This is why concentration is best achieved in a quiet room and why drivers often turn the radio down when they have to concentrate on complicated tasks that require more thinking than 'normal' driving does – for example, reversing or reading a complex series of road signs. However, 'normal' driving and activities such as typing and hand-eye co-ordination are handled by a different part of the brain, which is why we find it easy to think about sentences as we type and edit them, and why we can drive and hold an intelligent conversation at the same time.

If the goal of dictation software is 100% accuracy, is achieving perfection a laudable but misguided goal, when the real problem seems to be how to enable thinking and working at the same time and how to work without disturbing anyone? No way is saying 'back ... back ... back ... highlight forwards to the end of the word and delete' quicker than doing it with a mouse and keyboard – a fact that can easily be tested.

On a more fundamental level, Professor Shneiderman believes that human-human interaction is a poor model for computers to follow. 'We have a natural, rather childlike desire to see the human form and human behaviours in everything,' he explains, citing examples such as 'smiling' cars and anthropomorphic robots.

Hollywood images of sentient, talking computers such as HAL in Stanley Kubrick's *2001* have provided appealingly futuristic aspirations for the 'artificial intelligentsia', but Shneiderman believes they may be misguided in thinking that this is how people should communicate with machines in the future. 'Speech is the bicycle of user interfaces,' he says. 'It works, it's useful for people with disabilities and it can be used on the telephone where there's a big role for it; but it should really be the interface of last resort.'

Of course, the artificial intelligentsia and speech recognition researchers will press on with their work and will doubtless assure us that all we need is better technology to achieve the dream of computers that can understand all the subtleties of human communication. But for a computer to match the full range of human understanding will take a Herculean effort and billions of dollars of investment. And all of this will be wasted if people still feel self-conscious talking to a machine.

Push gets the shove

Internet browsers such as Netscape Navigator and Internet Explorer have become the standard way to interact with the World Wide Web, but in their infancy the digerati were confidently declaring them dead and buried, along with the very notion that internet users would actually have to exert themselves looking for information. 'Smooch your cranky old browser one last time, because it's going bye-bye,' panted *Wired* magazine in a particularly breathless cover story from March 1997. The next big thing? 'Push' technology!

The big idea was that instead of clicking around websites to find information, Push technology would send us what we wanted – or what we had already chosen to receive. Companies such as PointCast produced client software that acted rather like a screensaver, displaying information such as stock quotes and news updates that were being pushed to PCs in offices around the world. Simply check the screen for interesting headlines, click on them and be whisked away to a new page on which the full story would be told.

Today, however, browsers are still very much alive and Push's big idea has largely failed – at least in the form of a mass-market news and information screen envisaged by PointCast back in 1996. The problem was that for many users, the information being pushed to them was largely irrelevant and distracting. Instead of wasting time surfing around the net for information, they were now wasting time clicking on links and looking at things that were only marginally useful, like stock quotes and sports news (remember, they were surfing in company time!). Another, more serious, problem was that in many companies tens or even hundreds of workers had signed up for Push services; the result was that valuable bandwidth was being clogged up. Sending anything out of the building was like blowing into the wind.

But the underlying ideas of Push technology survive, albeit in contexts that we might not recognize as the Push we knew and loved before our IT departments told us to get it off our computers. AOL's Instant Messenger chat software includes the option to display a small ticker tape of news headlines and stock prices (American only!). We sign up for daily or weekly digests or newsletters that are emailed to us according to preferences we have already set. What's more, the emergence of SMS has opened up a new market for Push-style text alerts including pop gossip, sports scores and news headlines. PointCast itself has morphed into Infogate and offers a more streamlined version of the PointCast service for clients such as *USA Today*, which promotes it as a subscription-based service called NewsTracker. What the case of Push illustrates is that innovations rarely fail completely – they simply fail to find the right context or market at the right time.

NOTES

1 Liebowitz and Margolis' paper generated a lot of controversy and their article in *Reason* magazine attracted a detailed letter of rebuttal from Randy Cassingham, author of *The Dvorak Keyboard*.

2 Like human contact, silence and periods of quiet contemplation are something else that technologists seem intent on destroying.

Is shopping rational?

'*Supermarkets are about to be severely beaten up by online grocery stores, especially by WebVan.com.*'

Frank Feather
Futurist and author of *FutureConsumer.com*

The last few years have seen great innovation in the ways we can shop. Instead of just visiting the local high street or buying from catalogues, we can watch product demonstrations on numerous TV shopping channels, order electronically over the internet, through interactive TV and even using our mobile phones – some of which double up as wallets and allow payments that go through our phone bills. The arrival of new players such as Amazon and eBay has spurred bricks and mortar retailers into rethinking their relationships with customers, forcing them to take to the internet and open up new channels to the buying public. Innovative models such as Priceline's 'Name Your Own Price', mySimon's price comparison service or the collective buying of LetsBuyIt have given consumers an unprecedented choice in how they spend their hard-earned cash on the pleasures and necessities of life.

At the same time, high streets and shopping malls have experienced changes of their own. In the UK, two of the biggest success stories of recent years have been branded coffee shops such as Starbucks and mobile phone outlets like the Carphone Warehouse and The Link (though the market seems to be reaching saturation point).

SHOP TO LIVE, LIVE TO SHOP

E-tail entrepreneurs have often used the argument that shopping over the internet will free up our time so we can devote it to doing things we enjoy. The cash-rich, time-poor dotcommers who were working all hours to revolutionize the way we shop may have been too busy to go out and do it themselves, but back in the real world it seems that the rest of us were really quite content with the crowds and the queues and the bustle. So even though we have an alternative, it seems we're reluctant to give up the habit of a lifetime and do all our shopping online.

Earlier I described the coffee shop revolution as an environmental clue and I believe many dotcom entrepreneurs overlooked its significance. It isn't so much a sign that the Brits have finally come to appreciate a decent cup of latte, what it's really telling us is that high streets and malls are places of leisure. Far from being a time-consuming chore, shopping is the UK's favourite leisure activity. We work hard to earn our money, so why not enjoy the experience of spending it? Why reduce a complex, enjoyable and satisfying ritual to a few keystrokes on a computer? Why deny us the pleasure of going out and interacting, searching and finding, touching and feeling, trying on and handing over the cash so we can take possession of something that will make us feel better?

It's not that online shopping is a bad idea – quite the opposite. Companies

'Retail outlets and malls are bending over backwards to turn shopping from something that is functional into something that is more like visiting a theme park. There isn't a chance that companies using the internet to sell products will ever be able to match this and the idea that people will give it all up and shop in virtual reality using 3D avatars is naïve.'

Dr Sue Eccles
Lecturer in Marketing, University of Lancaster

such as Boo.com and WebVan may have gone spectacularly bust but the underlying concept of ordering things like groceries online and having them delivered is amazingly smart (and a potential boon to the elderly and disabled), just as catalogue shopping was before it. The problem is that catalogue shopping never really challenged the real thing, even though the real thing involves travelling to the shops, finding somewhere to park, fighting through the crowds, lugging the shopping around, queuing, paying and getting it all home. To argue that the advantage of online shopping is that it spares us all of these hassles is to undersell the true nature of its innovation. In many ways, online shopping is such a clever idea that you can only appreciate how smart it is by appreciating the *genius* that is the modern high street store.

THE SCIENCE OF STORES

Modern stores and supermarkets are not just thrown-together assemblages of food, clothes or gadgets stacked willy-nilly on rows of shelves. They are the products of 30 years of deeply insightful research into the foibles of how people behave in the real world. Since the 1970s, retail anthropologists have been following shoppers around, noting and filming every movement, every glance and every action they take. Their findings have shaped the modern shopping experience we know – and more importantly enjoy – today. Every aspect of a modern supermarket, from the positioning of the baskets to the height of the shelves, is the result of painstaking observation of what people do when they shop. By carefully analyzing the behaviour of people wandering around stores, retail anthropologists have been able to advise store owners how to make shopping easier and more enjoyable so that shoppers keep coming back for more of the same, pleasurable experience of spending money.

The guru of retail anthropology is Paco Underhill, founder of the New York consultancy Envirosell. His book, *Why We Buy: The science of shopping* is the bible of consumer behaviour and how it affects (or should affect) the layout of the modern retail store. Here are a few of the insights he has gained from more than two decades of following people around as they shopped:

- Spending is directly related to time spent in a store and that depends on how comfortable and enjoyable it is for the consumer.
- The worst place to put baskets is immediately inside the door. This is because people hurry in from the car park and need a 'landing strip' to slow down and adjust to their new surroundings.
- People will buy more if they are given a basket, but baskets also limit how much people will carry.
- Products for older people should be positioned where they can reach them conveniently, not on the lowest shelves. Products for children should be placed lower down, at their height, not high up.
- Most people are right-handed and this affects how you stack the shelves. The best-sellers should be conveniently placed so a person of average height can pick them up.
- People walk towards the right of the store, slow down for mirrors but generally face forwards. All of these affect how you position and display goods.
- People don't like being brushed against when they're shopping, so the aisles have to be wide enough to avoid 'butt brush'. Goods don't do well in narrow aisles for this reason.
- Men are cavalier shoppers, especially when given a vehicle (a shopping trolley) to drive around the supermarket. Men also don't like to ask for directions in a shop.

Much of this is the kind of common sense that has to be pointed out to you before you realize it!

From the e-tailer's point of view, the reason that online shopping is so smart is that these real world design issues simply *do not matter*. Nor do e-tailers have to spend money on shopping trolleys, security cameras, land for parking cars, pleasant-looking design, staff uniforms, ambient music or the fake aroma of freshly baked bread wafting across the bakery.

Of course, they are faced with different challenges such as interface design, database management, warehouse design, logistics and the challenge of making the online experience the best it can be, which is a significant and expensive undertaking in itself. But the theory behind e-tailing was that it ought to be cheaper to set up a single website and warehouse combination than operate a chain of shops.

Unfortunately for the likes of WebVan, that turned out to be a dangerous assumption because it relied far too heavily on consumers changing deeply ingrained behaviours in a hurry. Open a grocery store and people will buy from you simply because they live across the street. How many grocery stores could you have opened for the $800 million WebVan raised in finance before it went bust? But open an internet site and you have to spend millions advertising it, building a brand, building people's trust and getting them to return time and time again. That means you're funding their education, their apathy and their journey of discovery as they finally take the plunge and shop online. Even then, you've no guarantee they'll ever come back.

From the consumer's point of view, online shopping is a great leveller. As long as you have access to the internet (which admittedly isn't cheap), you can shop at any time, from anywhere, whether you're male, female, old, young, tall, short, dressed, undressed or sitting in a wheelchair. In this respect, all consumers are equal online – there's no lifting, no carrying, no bending down or reaching for the highest shelves and no physical limit to what you can put in a virtual shopping basket. You don't have to take the pesky kids along. What's more, you can search for the best prices at numerous price comparison sites and read product reviews at places like Amazon or epinions.com.

Add all of these advantages to the fact that shoppers also save on uncosted activities such as travelling, parking and queuing, and for consumers at least online shopping (particularly grocery shopping) looks like the no-brain innovation of all time. So why have people been so reluctant to take the plunge?

BAD TECHNOLOGY OR BAD EXPERIENCE?

One possible explanation comes from BTexact Technology's resident futurist, Ian Pearson. He says:

'Grocery shopping is inherently dull and boring and people don't really want to go out very often and do it. If you can find a good way to do it online, I believe people will convert, but making it good and easy to use over the internet is not trivial. A lot of companies that try to do it have got bad websites and some have lousy distribution.'

'But the main reason people haven't taken it up is that it takes ages to log on to the net and when they get access to it quite often the web is clogged up and it takes forever. At the moment it's a lot faster to get into your car and go to the supermarket than it is to shop online. That's why it hasn't taken off as predicted – it's down to the speed of the network and the design of the websites. If you have good websites and a fast network I think you'll see people using them quite a lot, but we're talking in a few years from now.'

Apart from the debatable assertion that grocery shopping is 'dull and boring', it's still framing the problem in technological terms – namely that smarter databases, faster connections and more powerful computers are all that's needed to solve the problem. Certainly all of these will help online shopping, but are they technological solutions that misunderstand the true nature of shopping? Can better technology compensate for the loss of the experience of shopping?

One important aspect of the experience of shopping is touch. Paco Underhill observes that shopping is one of the few human activities in which we deliberately set out to handle and examine things:

'A great deal of our first-hand experience of the world comes to us via shopping. Where else do we go with the specific intention of examining objects? To museums, of course, but don't try touching anything that's not in the gift shop – a retail environment. Stores alone are abundant with chances for tactile and sensory exploration. Even if we didn't buy things, we'd need to get out and touch and taste them once in a while.'

Madame Tussaud's, the famous London waxworks, used to have a policy of roping off its effigies to keep the public at a respectful distance. Then some bright spark decided that visitors might enjoy interacting with the 'celebrities' – standing next to them and posing for photographs.

Sure enough, the tourists loved it, which is why they queue every day to get in so they can be photographed next to the Queen or Bono.

Of course, you could open a virtual Tussaud's on the net with 3D representations of the waxworks and have a system whereby you scan in your own picture and composite yourself next to Arnie or Madonna. It would save you travelling to Madame Tussaud's and queuing to get in but would it be as much fun? I doubt it. What many e-tail entrepreneurs seem to have overlooked is that for many people shopping is as much fun as visiting an attraction like Tussaud's. They will put up with the travelling and the queues because the experience is so enjoyable.

Can technology solve the avocado problem?

What do online grocery stores tout as their big advantages? Convenient ordering from any desktop PC or even your mobile internet device? Delivery at a time that suits you? Low prices because they don't have the overheads of a store? Secure ordering with great order tracking? Intelligent agents to track your preferences and build up a convenient shopping list for when you next log in?

Now imagine you're making guacamole and you want some avocados. Not just any avocados – they have to be ripe. Which of the features above is most important to you now? Would you compromise on ripeness for ease of ordering or delivery, or for low prices or great order tracking?

Could technology make the experience better? What about a tele-immersive system in which you don some computer screen glasses and a pair of tactile feedback gloves and log on to a webcam that sits above the avocado display. You could squeeze the avocados virtually using the tactile gloves to control a super new robotic arm that's so sensitive and lifelike it would translate the gentlest squeeze and the merest squidge so you could truly fondle the fruit and pick the ones you want!

Would throwing all of that technology at the problem really make the experience more compelling? Would it tempt you to adopt the innovation of VR-enabled internet shopping? Or is it just gadgetry for the sake of it, dreamed up by some naïve technologist who ought to get out of the laboratory more often?

What if the same technology was developed for bomb disposal? Would that be naïve?

HYPE AND EXCITEMENT

Touching and examining are just part of an experience that taps into some pretty primeval emotions, according to marketing expert Jeremy Baker of London Guildhall University. He says many e-tail entrepreneurs failed because they didn't understand the true nature of shopping: 'When you buy a car you're buying much more than a means to get from A to B; when you buy a dress you're buying much more than clothing,' he explains. 'Shopping has hype, excitement, sexuality, expectation and a sense that you're in control; these are all primitive emotions. There is a real pleasure and a primeval sense of being a hunter-gatherer – going out into the world and coming back laden with goods.'

The question he thinks the dotcom entrepreneurs should have been asking is this: does online shopping engage those feelings and emotions, or does it merely address the functional act of ordering? 'If you believe shopping should be reduced to a technological experience you are very much mistaken,' he says.

TRANSACTING ISN'T SHOPPING

For most people, shopping is much more than just transacting. It is an elaborate activity that encompasses culture, habit, emotion, power, self-identity and social interaction. Dr Helen Woodruffe-Burton, a lecturer in marketing at the University of Lancaster, believes that many e-tailers failed to take these human foibles into account: 'They have overlooked what shopping means to a lot of people,' she says of their poor understanding of what is in reality a complex form of human behaviour.

'A lot of shopping behaviour is social. Having your friends with you and getting their feedback and approval is important, especially when you're buying clothes. Women want their husbands to see what they're buying and young girls often go into dressing rooms with their friends.'

In addition, shopping is a chance for families to bond in a common activity and an opportunity for children to learn skills and roles. Shopping for groceries is still very much a female activity and one in which the woman is in control: 'Even today, shopping is one of the few areas where women have the power,' says Dr Woodruffe-Burton. 'They are the decision-makers, they control the budget and so the internet is potentially a threat to that power. Going out shopping can be an escape.'

In escaping from the real world, many shoppers experience a blissful state known as 'flow' in which they become so in tune with what they're doing that they temporarily switch off from everything else. Many studies of flow have focused on intense activities such as rock climbing or creating works of art, but Dr Woodruffe-Burton believes it can happen during shopping trips as well. She suggests that flow encompasses many factors including the challenge of the shopping activity itself, the development and enjoyment of personal skills and the feeling of satisfaction when the job is done. Can you lose yourself shopping online? Does it matter?

THE LOSS OF CONTEXT

One of the biggest problems with online shopping is the loss of context. Go into a store and your eyes will be able to take in dozens of lines of products in a single glance, all of them neatly displayed in the context of something else. Clothes can be mixed and matched with other garments to give an overall look on a display, while items such as groceries are stacked so you can see all the biscuits or all the ready meals as you scan the shelves. Trying to replicate this online is a challenge; list items on separate pages and all the clicking and jumping will put people off. Put all the products on one page and it becomes cumbersome. Would you put pasta meals on the same page as curries? They are next to each other in the chill cabinet.

In a supermarket, how many ready meals would you visually scan before choosing the Chicken Tikka Masala with Pilau Rice – 10, 20 perhaps? Do you really want to look at 20 ready meals on an internet site before you make your choice? What about the average confectionery counter at the local store – how many chocolate bars are there to tempt you? How could any internet site better a sweet counter for displaying a hundred different lines of sweets? It gets worse: if the average family shopping basket contains 50–80 different items, how many other products will you scan in the supermarket before you select the ones you want?

Here's the rub: when embarking on the weekly shopping trip, do you write a list of all the goods you want – remember there might be more than 50 items – or do you have a few specifics in mind like milk and coffee and just a vague idea for the rest? Do you decide in advance exactly what you'll buy or wait until you get into the supermarket and have a look round for what you fancy? For most people, grocery shopping is not task-driven and goal orientated – things like browsing and spontaneity count. Indeed, spontaneity matters to the retailer too – and beyond – as Paco Underhill observes in his book:

'If impulse purchasing stopped, the economy would collapse.'

But the fact is that buying 50 of anything on the internet is a tough assignment. In objective terms, it may not be as time-consuming as actually going to the shops, but that's not the point. Just imagine trying to buy 50 books from Amazon using its search function and One-Click ordering – and that's internet shopping at its best! If you're a list-maker then fine, but if buying 50 items over the internet even *seems* daunting, that may be all it takes for the consumer to log off and head for the shops.

Of course, any intelligent shopping system will track your purchases from week to week and build up convenient lists of favourites that you can simply tick on subsequent trips. But if you tried to buy a full trolley of goods on your first online shopping trip and found the experience off-putting, you may never have returned to give the list bots the chance to make your life easier. This, of course, was eminently testable.

WHY WEBVAN FAILED

The belief that trips to the supermarket are a dreadful chore that ought to be automated out of existence features prominently in the initial public offering (IPO) prospectus of WebVan, the online grocer that went bankrupt in July 2001 despite having raised more than $800 million in funding from a lot of very smart investors.

WebVan was launched in 1999 by former bookshop entrepreneur Louis Borders, with the intention of shaking up America's low-margin grocery industry. (It's ironic that he never revolutionized the book-selling industry like Amazon's Jeff Bezos did, which proves that innovators are often outsiders!) Borders' plans were ambitious – remember, these were times for big bets: start from scratch, build automated warehouses in major cities and run a fleet of vans to deliver the goods at the customer's convenience.

When it came to market, WebVan's IPO prospectus reflected its founder's confidence in the online grocery model:

'Traditional store-based supermarkets face many challenges in providing a satisfying shopping experience for consumers. Physical space availability in stores limits the number of products supermarkets can offer and reduces merchandizing flexibility. This forces traditional store-based supermarkets to limit their product selection to the most popular products, further impairing customer selection. Traditional grocery retailers also face significant costs associated with building and operating large brick and mortar stores, including costs associated with personnel, real estate, construction, store set-up, inventory and fixed assets. The challenges facing these traditional retailers have created an opportunity for online grocery retailers to provide a more compelling and cost-effective solution. The internet provides a medium that could significantly improve the consumer grocery shopping experience.'

Many commentators have since accused the company of hubris and plain bad thinking, much of which is evident in the passage above. Traditional supermarkets have been serving customers for decades and, with the help of Paco Underhill and his ilk, they have refined the shopping experience into something that feels more like a day at a theme park. The reason many larger outlets have a 'limited' number of lines – around 30–40,000 – is probably because experience has told them that's all they need for a successful business. Could WebVan really differentiate itself profitably by carrying twice as many lines so that one customer in a thousand could choose exactly the right brand of extra virgin olive oil from a particular producer in Greece? As to providing a significant improvement on the grocery shopping experience, the customers obviously voted with their wallets and stuck with the old, inconvenient and gloriously irrational method of getting into the car and going to the supermarket. In the year 2000, although WebVan notched up an impressive $178 million in sales, serving 750,000 customers in seven cities, it also racked up losses of $453 million. A few months later, in July 2001, WebVan announced it was to close. It was the most spectacular failure of the dotcom bubble.

In an article in the online newsletter *Knowledge@Wharton*, Professor Robert Mittelstaedt of Wharton Business School suggested that WebVan had made some heroic assumptions about consumers and the industry itself that turned out to be hopelessly wrong. It overestimated the speed at which consumers would migrate to online shopping and underestimated how attached they were to their regular supermarket routines. WebVan's inclusion in its prospectus of a Forrester Research projection of an online grocery market worth $10.8 billion by 2003 also showed it was far too trustful of growth market forecasts that have historically proved optimistic. In 2001, Forrester revised the figure to $5.8 billion (see box opposite).

In addition, it believed that an upstart company could enter the market and build a completely new infrastructure of warehousing and delivery from scratch. (Amazon made a similar assumption, although its distribution to the customer was far simpler – the mail!)

In the same *Knowledge@Wharton* article, Wharton marketing professor Jerry Wind summed up WebVan's failure:

How the online grocery market looked in 2001

In November 2001, Forrester Research revised its previous forecast of a $10.8 billion online market for groceries in 2003 to the more conservative figure of $5.8 billion, although it also forecast the market would grow to $23.5 billion by 2006. Intriguingly, they also forecast that the growth in online grocery shopping will not mirror the growth in broadband penetration in the US, so the idea that all that's needed for e-commerce to take off is faster pipes may be misguided!

The same survey revealed some interesting customer attitudes towards online grocery shopping. When asked why they had stopped shopping online, 49% said traditional stores were cheaper and 29% preferred to visit them instead of shopping online. In a separate question for people who hadn't already bought groceries online, 44% said they enjoyed visiting a store and 35% didn't see the benefit of shopping online! Just 3% cited poor technology as the reason they would not buy online!

Source: *Online Grocery's Second Wind*
Forrester Research, 2001

'WebVan had the arrogance to think it could conquer the world. Money was cheap and venture capitalists were willing to fund any dumb idea. But primarily WebVan forgot to look at consumer behaviour, and it forgot basic economics.'

In the wake of WebVan's demise, the world's most successful online grocer is Tesco.com, the online arm of the long-established UK chain. Refusing to be caught up in the hype or make overly optimistic assumptions about human behaviour, Tesco played a more cautious game, using its existing supermarkets as picking centres and testing the concept at a small number

'Online grocery could easily get to 10% of the market. The key question is not what level it is going to get to, but when. It could take 20 years, it could take three years. It's the timing that people get wrong.'

John Browatt, CEO Tesco.com
Interviewed in the *Sunday Times*, September 2001

of outlets before taking its online shopping service to the rest of the country. In the year to March 2002, it sold groceries worth £356 million – not bad for an old economy dinosaur that didn't get it!

PRACTICAL RESISTANCE TO SHOPPING ONLINE

Apart from the kinds of barriers to online shopping that sociologists and psychologists have identified, other more tangible reasons for consumer resistance have scuppered many an innovative e-tailing business plan like WebVan's. Many of these may seem a little capricious, but remember, it's the consumer's perception that counts, not the objective reality:

- **Price:** Sometimes it's cheaper to shop in the high street, as the Forrester Research survey discovered.
- **Involvement** is still a major barrier for many people. Some goods, such as books and CDs are relatively low involvement. Although Amazon doesn't let you flick through its books (there are excerpts of some on its website), it compensates for this loss of involvement by adding editorial and user reviews. On its music site you can listen to clips of the more obscure artists far more easily than you can in a record shop. Clothes demand higher involvement, as do TV sets, hi-fis, cars and furniture. With many of these kinds of goods, people are proving themselves more than willing to research on the net and buy in the real world (or vice

versa), which doesn't exactly help dotcoms if all they're doing is providing information for no sale in return.

- **Security** is still a major concern. It seems irrational, but shoppers who think nothing of handing their Amex to a waiter in a restaurant to be processed out of sight are still reluctant to send their credit card details over a web page encrypted so securely that even a teenager would have problems cracking it.

- **Delivery** also seems to be an issue. Many people don't like to be tied to a particular delivery window, even if they can specify it several days in advance so they know they're going to be at home. Again, this may appear irrational but ask your friends and it's a factor that will pop up time and time again. I can best describe this reluctance as 'Oh, I just can't be bothered to wait in', because that's how numerous people have described it to me! The same people have no conceptual problem with taking half a day off work to wait for a new washing machine to be delivered!

- **Impatience** is an intriguing factor for which I've yet to hear a decent unifying theory. Although you can order goods over the internet, the shopping process isn't really complete until you've received them. So how quickly do you want to take delivery?

Pizzas are time-sensitive because they fill an immediate need and go cold. Books don't, so we seem happy to wait a couple of days for Amazon to deliver, rather than go to the bookshop – in which case we'd probably get the book sooner. Prescription drugs are the kinds of things you want immediately, not tomorrow or the day after. If you'd lived in New York during the dotcom boom you could have had snacks and books delivered within the hour by Kozmo or UrbanFetch, but both of those companies flopped, having burned through around $300 million in venture capital. (Their backers obviously believed they were more than just courier companies selling low-margin goods and delivering them largely at their own expense – I guess they must have seen something the rest of us missed!)

Some people who want to buy a mobile phone will wait until the weekend to visit a store, even though they could order it online midweek and have it delivered on Saturday morning. Others will shop in a buying collective such as LetsBuyIt and are prepared to wait up to three weeks, as long as they can get a discount. Despite its innovative model, LetsBuyIt's sales figures suggest that most people probably won't delay gratification too long for a discount, or that you might find it difficult to build a viable business serving those that will.

On the other hand, the success of the online auctioneer eBay shows that people will delay gratification for items that are unusual or hard to find. If you want a rare CD or some *Blade Runner* memorabilia, eBay is the best place to look, and you won't mind the wait because you place a high value on the item you're trying to buy.

- **Shipping costs** may be a factor for some people. One of the advantages of going to a shopping centre in the car is that all of the shipping costs are aggregated when you drive home.
- **Demographic factors** are important too. The reason that house prices are rising so much in the UK is the fact that more people are living alone. Single people are unlikely to place large grocery orders over the internet, especially if there is a minimum order size before the delivery becomes free. Being single, they probably enjoy meeting other people at the weekend when they shop, so again it's the social experience that is important to them. (In parts of London, upmarket supermarkets are reckoned to be great places to meet the opposite sex – just remember to put the right 'signalling' foods in the basket, such as a ready meal for one and a half bottle of decent wine!)

THE FUTURE OF SHOPPING

Check out Ian Pearson's website at BT and you'll find some entertaining visions of what the future of shopping might be – or at least what is technically possible. Apparently, you'll be able to navigate stores using GPS-enabled trolleys that will notify you of nearby offers and enable the store owner to reduce congestion when certain aisles fill up. Store lighting will highlight individual goods, while other products will be dimmed out if you've never shown any interest in them. There will be cyber zones where you can don a headset and shop in virtual reality, while the wonders of augmented reality will beam additional information and customer reviews to your eyeballs as you walk past the goods. Portable video terminals will allow you to bring your friends, even if they're miles away, on a video link. Personalization will increase and you'll be able to get a pair of trousers made for you, once your body has been scanned and converted into a 3D avatar that you can then use to try on clothes on the net.

Back in the real world, however, the idea of using high-tech navigation systems around the aisles assumes that supermarkets have learned nothing from decades of retail anthropology and that store layouts are so poor that people need assistance getting round. It also assumes that shoppers don't learn where the goods are when they visit stores time and time again, and that they can't read the large signs overhead saying 'dairy produce' or 'pet foods'. Would a supermarket really invest in such a navigation system, given the intense competition and low margins inherent in the industry? Somehow I doubt it would pass any cost-benefit analysis; what possible value would it add to the customer's experience?

The idea of augmented reality is based on the notion that people are unhappy with the information content of the real world and want more, which is a doubtful premise for the vast majority of the human race. We are shoppers, not fighter pilots. It also implies that grocery packaging carries insufficient information and that people want to learn more, which again is a rather dubious assumption given that people rarely study the information already there, other than to see how many calories there are in their curry. In fact, studies show that many people can't even tell you the price of something they've just put in their basket.

Anyway, the information content of the average supermarket is already huge, because of all the different product lines, the colourful packaging and the promotional signage round the place. Why add to the noise? Probably because the technologists who tout such ideas tend to overestimate the amount of information the rest of us want to consume. People are already complaining that they have too much information to cope with in the digital age, but the visionaries want to give us even more, and not in the office – in the shops and in our leisure time!

IF YOU DISCOUNT IT, WILL THEY COME?

One of the most dangerous assumptions of the dotcom boom was the idea that if you offer a lower price than everyone else, buyers will turn up in droves. E-tailers made the mistake of thinking that all consumers were price sensitive, whoever they were or whatever they were buying. Sadly, for many innovative e-tailing businesses, that turned out not to be the case.

That's not to say shoppers don't like keen prices, they do – just look at the Harrod's sale and the success of Wal-Mart. But the price we pay is just one part of a shopping experience that encompasses trust and the assurance that if anything goes wrong it will be rectified. In the case of the co-buying site LetsBuyIt, for example, the issue was whether shoppers would wait a couple of weeks to receive their goods in return for a discount.

According to Professor Sarah Maxwell, of the Fordham University Pricing Center in New York, many e-tailers made a big mistake when they set out to offer lower prices instead of emphasizing factors such as the ease of ordering online and home delivery. These were, after all, times when people felt optimistic and affluent, and valued time and convenience more than money. 'I think they shot themselves in the foot,' she says of the aggressive discounting strategies many e-tailers used to build up a customer base. Price cutting, she argues, was a 'dumb idea' that took over the internet: 'They were shouting *cheap* when they should have been shouting *convenient* and emphasizing what a wide selection they had.'

Many shoppers were unwilling to do business with unknown e-tailers just because they were offering a lower price. What they wanted was reliability – and remember that many people were already wary of passing their credit card details over the net for fear of hackers. For this reason, e-tailers had to spend fortunes on marketing to buy a reputation for being trustworthy and reliable. Bricks and mortar retailers didn't have this problem. If your goods were faulty, you could return them to the store for a refund. They also had deeper pockets to fund price wars.

Another problem for e-tailers was that they created an unrealistic expectation of lower prices right across the internet, says Professor Maxwell. Economists call this 'reference pricing' and shoppers use the reference price as a mental benchmark against which to judge what they should be paying for goods. E-tailers weren't exactly helped by price comparison sites that allowed web shoppers to hunt for the cheapest price among a number of merchants. Price comparison is great for shoppers because it encourages price competition, but it's bad news for online merchants who are trying to turn a profit – a fact that many investors seem to have completely ignored.

By setting reference prices in the mind of the consumer at 10–15% below the high street price, many e-tailers found it difficult to retain customers when the discounting strategies of 'land grab' turned to the more realistic pricing policies of 'path to profits' and the prices had to rise to more sustainable levels. At this point, the new entrants were no longer competing on the basis of price and all the other factors like trust, reliability and service once again became important factors for consumers – assuming they weren't already. In fact, in 2001, Forrester Research reported that many grocery shoppers had deserted online stores because goods were actually cheaper in the supermarket!

LOCATION, LOCATION, LOCATION

Another shopping innovation being touted around over the past few years is the idea of offering shoppers electronic coupons based on their location, using position-fixing technologies developed for mobile phones. This, of course, assumes that people will not be annoyed by being buzzed with discount coupons every few minutes as nearby businesses try to tempt them in. It also assumes that shoppers will walk out of their way to get a discount – an activity known as 'price searching' – but studies of petrol stations suggest that motorists can rarely be bothered to drive around in order to find the lowest price because there is a trade-off between effort expended and money saved. Professor Maxwell says: 'Generally people will not search as much as you think they will. They won't go very far at all for a discount.'

Wireless price comparison services may flounder for exactly this reason, although canny shoppers may use them to negotiate discounts with the merchant in whose shop they're standing, having compared all the locally available alternatives. But if all the rival shops in a location publish real time pricing details, it might lead to a flattening of prices – as happens in any market – because the shops themselves could use the pricing information to price their goods accordingly. If that turns out to be the case, the very technology designed to identify price differences will end up destroying them, although consumers should benefit.

Trials of location-based discounting have taken place at major shopping centres in the UK but failed to generate sufficient interest – or business – for the shops taking part. Setting up a location-based discount alerting service requires a lot of infrastructure: it needs a system whereby a mobile phone's position can be fixed with a fair degree of precision and some way of signing up and 'geocoding' the retailers so the system knows where they are. Then the whole thing requires the intelligence to figure out where shoppers are, match them to local retailers and send them a message saying they can get money off at a shop nearby. The shop also needs some method of identifying and registering shoppers who have taken up the discount so its owners can measure how successful the promotion has been.

Alternatively, the shop could stick a 10% off sign in the window, which would catch the attention of everyone going by – and at a fraction of the cost. Why complicate matters?

DOES MY BUM LOOK BIG IN THIS?

There are some interesting and much-hyped technologies being tested on certain clothing websites to help make it easier to shop for clothes over the internet – or so their developers claim.

My Virtual Model is an attempt to create a 3D avatar roughly corresponding to what you look like, so that you can try on virtual clothes in stores like Lands End and Blair. In a study of the system between November 2000 and April 2001, Lands End claimed that shoppers who used the avatar were 26% more likely to buy clothes than those who didn't, and they spent 13% more.

Having tried the system myself, I didn't find it compelling enough to use because the avatar looked nothing like me. I'd have rather seen the clothes on a real model so I could at least delude myself I'd look as good in them. I don't aspire to look like a character from *The SIMS* and I doubt many other people do either – we want to look like the folks in the Calvin Klein ads! When I buy a surfer shirt, I want to imagine I'm some cool dude on the beach, not be reminded that I'm an out of shape 41-year old who needs to use the Water Rower a bit more often.

I suppose you could personalize avatars by adding a photo of your own face and mapping it over the head of the model to make it look more realistic. But of course, it wouldn't look more realistic would it? Anyway, when looking at images of themselves, people generally fall into two categories: they're either vain (in which case they'll hate looking at a 3D cartoon with their own head superimposed on top) or they hate looking at pictures of themselves (ditto).

Another way to personalize avatars is to scan your entire body, and companies such as Cyberscan have developed body scanners exactly for this purpose. The big idea is that you'll be able to order a personalized pair of jeans to fit *you*. On a commercial level, scanning thousands of different people certainly will give manufacturers an idea of typical body shapes so they can tweak the clothes to make them fit better. Humanity is, after all, getting fatter. But with chains like Gap and Levi's offering so many leg/waist/fit variations you have to ask how much better the options could be? Sure, it's not bespoke, but it's *good enough*, and sometimes things that are good enough will beat innovations that try to be perfect. (Humanity's desire for personalization is something else that technologists always seem to overestimate.) And then, of course, there's the small matter of the economics of producing custom-made jeans …

Much has been written about the use of body scanners and avatars so you can dress yourself over the internet but, again it's likely that the vanity angle will rear its ugly head. There's a famous British comedy sketch in which a woman simply asks: 'Does my bum look big in this?' The people developing 'dress-your-own-avatar' technology ought to watch it and think about what it really means.

Firstly, it shows that women are concerned about body image; the prospect of seeing an accurately rendered 3D model of all their imperfections is unlikely to prove popular. (For some reason, we don't seem to mind looking in mirrors – which will show off all our imperfections in glorious real life high resolution images – because that's normal!) Secondly, the question implies that women seek reassurance about how they look, and that in turn emphasizes the social aspects of shopping and the importance of feedback and approval. Internet shopping is usually a lonely affair; how many friends can you fit around the computer?

That's not to say body scanners, avatars and 3D-rendered clothing are a bad idea – just think of all the possibilities in computer games, scanning yourself in and fighting alongside Lara Croft. Accurate body mapping and the realistic rendering of clothes are the holy grails of computer animation and they'll undoubtedly improve computer games and animated films beyond all recognition. Again, so far, it's a question of wrong context, wrong market.

In the world of commerce, companies such as Pulse Entertainment in the US and BTexact are developing avatar reps to give out information on websites, but their success will depend on whether potential customers find them as appealing as Shrek or as annoying as Jar Jar Binks!

If avatars have any future in shopping it may be that instead of shopping *from* them or *using* them, we shop *for* them. Already, multiplayer online worlds such as Entropia and Habbo enable visitors to create avatars so they can interact with each other using chat technology. In the Habbo Hotel, you can create your own room and furnish it with virtual furniture in exchange for real money. Surely the next step will be to offer avatar fashion shops so you can treat your alter ego to some funky new outfits to make sure they (or you!) stand out from the crowd.

But back in the real world, can you *really* see a woman pointing to a computer-generated dress and asking: 'Does my avatar's bum look big in this?'

Delivering the goods

As the internet bubble was deflating, a couple of entrepreneurs were hawking a plan around London to raise money for a home delivery service serving local communities. The market opportunity, they claimed, was that Tesco.com didn't do same day deliveries; nor would it deliver stuff like movies or take-away foods.

What they planned to do was start in London and enrol local shops – grocers, take-aways, wine shops, video stores and the like – and put them all on to one website so you could order everything you wanted in one go, wherever you were. Their back-end logistics would take care of fulfilling the order from all the different shops in each area and a taxi would whizz round, pick it all up and deliver it to your door.

Does that sound like a logistical nightmare in the making? How much would it cost to visit and sign up a decent selection of shops and restaurants in a single area such as Putney in London? How would they spread the service to the whole of London and then the rest of the UK? How would they cope with the cataloguing and database management for all the different goods, meals, videos and bottles of wine and all the different prices being charged by different shops? How would orders be transmitted to the shops so they could be fulfilled – would the vendors have to be online all day? Who would bear the cost of equipping the shops with the computer and internet access? What if one vendor hadn't checked his email by the time the delivery taxi arrived? What advantage was there to doing it over the net? What was to stop people simply nipping out to the shops and buying the stuff themselves?

In the end, the entrepreneurs gave up, having failed to find any finance. Was it the downturn in the market that was to blame, or was it simply a bad idea?

Why innovation succeeds

*'A firm's inability to predict the success of its products
is often a costly liability.'*[1]

Tony Ulwick and John A Eisenhauer – Strategyn

Having spent the last 11 chapters thinking about the reasons why innovation fails, let's end on a more optimistic note and consider why it succeeds. Although this book isn't specifically about launching new products, it's an activity that has generated a lot of studies on what goes into a successful innovation.

So what can we learn from the gurus? Most studies tend to focus on the strategy, culture and execution of innovation, but a study published in 1999 suggests that the idea itself holds many clues to its future success. That may sound rather obvious, but sometimes the intuitively obvious needs some hard figures to back it up, and surprisingly few studies of innovation have looked at the problem from this angle.

CAN AN IDEA PREDICT ITS OWN SUCCESS?

According to authors Jacob Goldenberg, Donald Lehmann and David Mazursky, the answer is a resounding yes. In a working paper published by the Marketing Science Institute (MSI) in 1999, they suggest that the future success of an innovation can be predicted by studying the idea itself and the unique proposition that it implies. They argue:

'Because the greatest monetary loss for failed products comes at the market introduction stage, and since expenditures for developing a new product increase as the process advances toward launch, it is critical to screen out concepts and ideas that are likely to be failures early in the process.'

The hard figures they obtained came from looking at nearly 200 new products, including 111 successes and 86 failures.[2] Successful products had some or all of the following characteristics:

- they were moderately new to the market
- they were based on tried and tested technology
- they saved money, met customer needs and supported existing behaviours.

Conversely, the products most likely to fail were based on cutting edge or untested technology, followed a trend ('me too' products) or were created with no clear need or solution in mind (technology for the sake of it). Of 21 key success factors, those most highly associated with successful innovations were 'idea factors', which are summarized below.

'Need spotting' involves actively finding an answer to a problem, while 'solution spotting' involves finding a problem for a solution. An example of solution spotting is the use of lasers in CD and DVD players. The technology already existed and innovators found something new to do with it. 'Mental inventions' are those light bulbs that suddenly appear above your head and 'random events' are moments of pure serendipity when you stumble across an answer you weren't really looking for.

Source of the idea	Success (%)	Failure (%)
Need spotting	68.8	31.2
Solution spotting	87.5	12.5
Market research	80	20
Random event	92.9	7.1
Mental invention	27.7	72.3
Trend following	25	75

Source: MSI Working Paper Report No. 99–110, 1999

The authors claim that their model has the power to predict success and failure in about nine cases out of ten, which is a pretty good strike rate!

ROBERT COOPER'S STUDY OF PRODUCT DEVELOPMENT

Winning at New Products is probably the classic text on the development of new products and, as such, it focuses on the execution of the product development process and the culture of innovation within the organization. These, of course, can be controlled and optimized by the innovators themselves, thus increasing their own chances of success.

Based on his extensive studies of how new products are created, Professor Cooper identifies 15 factors crucial to success in product innovation. Among them are the following:

- Doing lots of homework to find out in advance what the consumer wants or what new opportunities you can offer them.
- Having a structured product development process with exacting criteria for progressing or killing the project.
- Creating a genuinely better and differentiated product that offers real benefits and tangible value, and is fully aligned with the needs of the customer and the market.
- Having an international outlook in design, development and marketing.
- Ensuring that the product has the backing of senior management and that the corporate culture is amenable to new ideas.
- Launching the product with adequate resources into an attractive and receptive market.

In his book, Professor Cooper describes a structured process – the Stage-Gate™ process – for new product development. The 'stages' are fairly logical:

- A **discovery** phase in which new ideas are identified or generated.
- A desk research phase called **scoping** to take a closer look at a potential project.

- A more detailed **business case** stage in which both market and technical factors are evaluated so that a detailed plan can be drawn up.
- **Design and development** of the innovation to turn it into a reality.
- **Testing and validation** to see if it works, if it can be built easily and, most importantly, to find out whether people want to buy it.
- Finally, there is the **launch** phase when production and marketing gear up and the product hits the shelves.

More importantly, perhaps, are the 'gates' that Cooper establishes to weed out bad ideas. At the end of each stage tough questions are – or should be – asked about the project, and its sponsors must justify why the innovation should be allowed to proceed. For each gate is a set of deliverables – goals or results agreed in advance, with clearly defined criteria which the innovation must meet if it is to survive. The gate reviews conclude with decisions on whether to kill the project or let it proceed. If the gate is hurdled successfully, resources for the next stage should be allocated and new goals agreed.

One of the advantages of having such a structured product development process, with clearly defined criteria agreed in advance and obvious to all concerned, is that it takes much of the bad thinking out of the process. Problems like ego involvement, groupthink, overconfidence and the inability to accept uncomfortable feedback can be eliminated and a bad project killed without bruising too many egos. Many large companies routinely use formalized processes; but inventors and people starting small businesses rarely impose such a structure on their own attempts to innovate, which is probably why so many of them fail.

THE FOUR MERITS OF INNOVATION

Having looked at the idea and the process by which it is turned into reality, what about the product itself? What clues does that hold to its success? Back in March 1978, the *Harvard Business Review* published a paper entitled *How to Spot a Technological Winner* in which the authors George White and Margaret Graham argued that successful innovations could be identified by looking at the power of the core technology and its implications for business. They isolated four success factors – the four merits of innovation:

- **Inventive merit:** The extent to which the innovation relieves or avoids the constraints of the existing way of doing things.
- **Embodiment merit:** Improvements in the physical form that allow full expression of the inventive merit.
- **Operational merit:** The extent to which the innovation simplifies existing practices.
- **Market merit:** The extent to which the other merits address or open up markets.

It's important to understand that each merit can be positive or negative: for example, the embodiment of an innovation can diminish the value of the technological innovation it contains; the operational aspects may add complexity that makes the innovation less attractive.

Let's take the Apple iPod MP3 player and the Segway Human Transporter (encountered in Chapter 5) as examples and look at the four merits of each.

APPLE iPOD

Inventive merit:	Using a small hard disk to store files instead of solid state memory greatly increases the amount of music that can be carried. Instead of 1–2 hours of music, it can carry the equivalent of 100 CDs. Furthermore, it can play for ten hours and be recharged quite quickly.
Embodiment merit:	The iPod is smaller than a pack of cards with a simple, touch-sensitive jog wheel and a menu-driven interface for easy access of tunes. Had the hard disk been much bigger, the embodiment merit would have diluted the inventive merit, which was to use a disk instead of solid state memory. Had it required bigger batteries, this too would have diluted the inventive merit.

Operational merit: Along with the iPod, Apple developed its iTunes software for people to record and organize music into convenient playlists on their computers. The use of a fast Firewire link and synchronization software enables the iPod to download automatically any new tunes that have been added since the last link-up, thus saving the user the hassle of transferring files manually. Had the download process been clumsy and time-consuming, this would have diluted the inventive and embodiment merits.

Market merit: The iPod's huge capacity, light weight, beautiful design, small size and ease of use have given the company a successful product for which it can charge a premium price. New markets have been opened up by the addition of a Windows-compatible version.

SEGWAY HUMAN TRANSPORTER

Inventive merit: The innovative use of gyroscopes enables the Segway to move as its rider directs it, simply by leaning backwards or forwards or from side to side. However, the gyroscopic technology is expensive and these costs must be passed on to the consumer.

Embodiment merit: The Segway has a simple platform on which the user stands, holding the handlebars to steer. The need for batteries means the machine weighs around 85lbs, which can be a disadvantage if the user needs to carry it up stairs – for example while commuting.

Operational merit: Simple and fun to use, people can step on and off it very easily, making it ideal for use in warehouses where it could improve the efficiency of pickers.

	Other markets might include local delivery services or theme parks where people want a fun way to get around.
Market merit:	A cost-benefit analysis in a warehouse situation might reveal that the value added was insufficient, compared with alternatives such as micro-scooters or sneakers. The high cost may put it out of the reach of most consumers, who may prefer to buy a bicycle or a motor scooter instead. What will consumers regard as the benefits of owning a Segway?

Clearly, the iPod is a winner on all fronts, combining a simple but compelling inventive merit with a pleasing embodiment and clear operational advantages. The case for the Segway is less clear – chiefly on the grounds of cost-benefit and its debatable advantages over cheaper alternatives.

Checking the iPod against the findings of Goldenberg and his colleagues earlier in the chapter, it's interesting to note that its inventive merit is not based on untested or cutting edge technology, unlike the Segway's innovative gyroscopic stabilizers. In addition, the Segway is new to the world – which increases its chance of failure – whereas the iPod is just new to the firm. Disk-based MP3 players already existed when the iPod was launched, and although it was clearly following a trend, its advantages were sufficiently attractive for people to rate it a 'must have' gadget compared with its rivals.

As to the source of the idea, the iPod was probably developed in response to a clear consumer need – namely, to be able to carry around much more music than was possible with existing devices. Looking at the Segway, it seems to have been much more inventor-generated – a case of a very brilliant and creative engineer thinking: 'This would be a great idea'. It remains to be seen whether enough people agree with him for the Segway to become a commercial success, let alone live up to the ridiculous hype it generated.

THINKING ABOUT THE USER

Looking at ideas, processes and products can offer many valuable insights into what makes a successful innovation, but understanding how the consumer will react to it is probably the most important insight of all.

In a seminal *Harvard Business Review* paper entitled *Knowing a Winning Business Idea When You See One*,[3] Professors W Chan Kim and Renée Mauborgne argue that innovators must create exceptional utility at a price that is both attractive to the consumer and profitable for themselves.

Innovations, they argue, are not just used, so to focus purely on ease of use is to miss much of the bigger picture. Instead, they emphasize the fact that there is an adoption process consisting of six important stages – what they call the 'buyer experience cycle':

Purchase:	How easy is it to research and buy the product? Can you make it any easier for the buyer? Is the transaction secure and trustworthy?
Delivery:	How good is the delivery service? Is the product easy to unpack and install? Just think of when you took delivery of your first desktop computer!
Use:	Is the product easy to use? Does it require training? Can it do the job properly? Does it require new behaviours?
Supplements:	Do you need anything else to make the product work – is it co-dependent? If so, are these supplements costly? Remember the Anoto wireless pen, which needs specially printed paper. For innovators of course, this is the classic razor scenario – sell them the razor and they'll have to buy the blades.
Maintenance:	Does the product need regular maintenance? How easy to upgrade is it? Apple and Microsoft have both introduced automatic update services that take the hassle out of keeping their operating systems up to date. Likewise, anti-virus software providers have similar offerings to keep PCs up to date with the latest virus definitions.

Disposal: What waste products does the product produce? Is the product itself easy to throw away? This is becoming an issue with consumer electronics, fridges, TVs and even plastic carrier bags!

Having identified six important stages in the buyer experience cycle, Kim and Mauborgne refine their model to add what they call the six 'utility levers' of the consumer, namely:

- productivity
- simplicity
- convenience
- risk
- fun and image
- environmental friendliness.

The important thing to understand is that these six utility levers can be pulled at each of the six stages of the buyer experience cycle. Kim and Mauborgne propose a 6 × 6 grid – the 'Buyer Utility Map' – in which innovators can plot and check their ideas at every stage of the cycle.

For example, Amazon's One-Click online ordering makes consumers more productive at the purchase stage of the cycle, it rates highly on simplicity and convenience and the delivery options allow packages to be received at home or at work. Ordering through Amazon is secure, which reduces the risks of transacting, and the company's returns policy allows customers to return books if they feel they have made a mistake buying them.

The PC manufacturer Dell has also pioneered online selling and its delivery options include installation at home by an engineer. For many people, having someone knowledgeable to set the computer up is a benefit worth paying for.

For innovators, the challenge is to think how they can make the consumer more productive, make their life simpler and more convenient, reduce their risks and let them enjoy themselves at every possible stage from purchase through to disposal. That's the key to success.

'Newly released products are often declared failures because of their inability to meet the criteria that define value in the eyes of the customer. It is at this point that companies often find out what criteria customers are using to judge the value of their products. One must ask, if these criteria can surface and be used to judge the value of a product shortly after its introduction, why can't they be uncovered and used to evaluate a product's potential the day before it is introduced? The week before? Six months before? More to the point, why can't they be uncovered before a product is conceptualized and used to help define the product itself?'

Tony Ulwick and John A Eisenhauer
Predicting the Success or Failure of a New Product Concept
Strategyn white paper

NOTES

1 *Predicting the Success or Failure of a New Product Concept.* Strategyn white paper.
2 *The Primacy of the Idea Itself as a Predictor of New Product Success*: MSI Working Paper, Report No. 99–110, 1999. Interestingly, some of their examples are drawn from Robert McMath's book, *What Were They Thinking?*, which we encountered in Chapter 6.
3 *Harvard Business Review*, September 2000.

Failure is an option*

'Trying is the first step towards failure.'

Homer Simpson, *The Simpsons*

'Taking risks is why we're out here.'

James T Kirk, *Star Trek*

THE HEALTHINESS OF NEGATIVITY

To many go-getting entrepreneurs it must seem unhelpful and downright perverse to write a book that seemingly revels in picking faults in somebody else's 'great ideas'. As I said earlier, surely we should be encouraging risk-taking, enterprise and visionary thinking, not knocking them.

But my point is this: things that seem like great ideas at the time can have disastrous consequences if we rush into them without thinking. That doesn't just apply to dotcom entrepreneurs, or the telco chiefs who blew billions buying 3G licences in the belief that we'll spend all our time surfing the internet on our mobile phones and buy flowers or books with them at every opportunity (you'd be amazed how many people trot out these two examples when they talk about the benefits of mobile internet!).

We are all innovators in our day to day lives. We make big decisions about

---

* Terms and conditions apply

moving home or changing career, and all of these decisions make perfect sense to us at the time. But when those decisions turn out bad, it's likely that we made the same mistakes as entrepreneurs who launched new ideas or new products that went on to fail. We didn't do our homework, we let our feelings get in the way of sound decision-making and we ignored all the evidence that suggested we might be about to make a big mistake.

Here's an experiment that will prove my point. The next time one of your friends comes up to you bubbling with enthusiasm because they've had some fantastic, life-changing idea, see how many awkward little questions you have to ask before they become really annoyed and accuse you of being negative and unhelpful. I'd be surprised if it takes more than three. That's because risk-taking, innovation and entrepreneurship are regarded as desirable and positive forces in our go-go capitalist society, and anyone who asks too many awkward questions is attacked as a doomsayer.

But if we are to improve our chances of creating successful innovations, it's important to understand that a certain amount of supportive scepticism is necessary to the process. Given the high failure rates of innovation, it's the critics and doomsayers who have the track record of being right, so why not take more notice of them? For many entrepreneurs, embracing the sceptics and recognizing their worth is a difficult cultural shift.

THE HEALTHINESS OF FAILURE

Like climbing mountains or exploring unknown lands, innovation is a risky business with high rewards for those who take the risks. It's a form of experimentation and, as in science, experiments that fail to produce any results can be just as valuable as those with more positive outcomes. The internet bubble was a period in which many experiments took place. Money was cheap and backers were willing to take risks – albeit with someone else's cash. New ideas and combinations were tried out, and we found that most of them didn't work. Although it may seem that huge amounts of money were squandered, the cash didn't just disappear into a black hole. It was spent on salaries, services and equipment that boosted the economy for a while. Sure, investors may have been burnt, but isn't that the risk of risk capital? The downside, of course, is that investors are now less willing to fund genuinely good ideas in these more sober and discriminating times.

> 'In order to get the 1–2% of really great things, maybe we need the 98–99% of failures. If we aren't failing at innovation, we aren't trying. In the US we have more success with start-ups because we tolerate failure more than other countries. In other cultures it can end your career.'
>
> Don Norman

Conventional wisdom tells us that we should admire the entrepreneurs who had the guts to try and fail because they were willing to risk everything to make those dreams come true. After all, innovation is the engine of a healthy economy and failure to innovate is most definitely not an option.

But here's an interesting question: in our enterprise culture where, as one venture capitalist put it, 'the only way to be a real failure is never to have tried', at what point does failure become unacceptable, and for what reasons? When NASA lost Mars Climate Orbiter it held a board of inquiry to establish what went wrong. Mistakes were identified, recommendations were made and lessons were learned. There was no board of inquiry after the collapse of WebVan or the CueCat or many of the dotcom era's more spectacular failures.

> 'Innovation for innovation's sake alone isn't good business. But innovation only for business's sake will be empty of the passion and creative genius necessary to turn a great idea into a great challenge. US business has proven time and time again that it knows how to fail. The challenge for the next decade is to figure out how to fail intelligently.'
>
> Michael Schrage
> *Harvard Business Review*, November 1989

To use the analogy of exploring, should we admire someone who sets out to conquer Mount Everest wearing a tweed jacket and hobnailed boots? Mallory and Irving tried it in the 1920s in a heroic but doomed attempt to reach the summit. They were true innovators who knew the risks and prepared as best they could. But if today's climbers set out ill-prepared and ill-equipped, ignoring obvious warnings about the dangers, should we admire their spirit and enterprise or should we condemn them for being reckless ego-trippers who shouldn't have even tried?

Clearly, there is a balance; too much critical analysis can lead to analysis paralysis and, sometimes, inspiration and gut feeling can make a mockery of conventional wisdom, just as some great success stories – like text messaging – have come from the most unpromising beginnings. But that's no excuse for avoiding the tough questions. Nor should entrepreneurs be too quick to deploy the rather hackneyed 'Walkman Defence' or the equally tired 'SMS Excuse', which is roughly that market research and critical thinking would have probably killed the Sony Walkman or the recent phenomenon of text messaging, so why should we bother?

Anyway, success and failure depend on time, space and perception; a failure now can be the basis of a huge success in the future, so should we even be concerned if things go wrong today?

Entrepreneurs argue that we shouldn't stigmatize or punish failure for fear of discouraging risk-taking in the future. In many cases that's probably

'Anyone who fails to innovate is not doing their job well. Being innovative is just fulfilling one's responsibility. Although failed innovations are very common, they are not a cause for penalties. The failure itself already serves that function. In contrast, those who fail to innovate are the ones who get penalized.'

Morris Chang
Chairman of Taiwan Semiconductor Manufacturing Company
Speaking in 1999 at the Digital Era Summit Forum

right because, as I've pointed out, great innovations can fail for reasons that can seem irrational and capricious. Even the best-prepared innovator can flunk.

On the other hand, should we reward the reckless entrepreneur or the disastrous chief executive with a pat on the back and a reassurance that failing doesn't matter, because what really matters is that they tried?

If innovators bring failure upon themselves, if they don't do basic market research or ignore compelling evidence that there is no market for their product, should we applaud them for having had a go? Should we admire the founders of failed dotcom companies who believed their own hype and were so full of hubris that they boasted how they were going to change our lives, when most of them hadn't bothered to find out what our lives were really like? Where should we draw the line?

The bubble may have been an aberration in which critical thinking was conveniently turned off on a massive and disastrous scale. But the truth is that long before it ever inflated, innovators were coming up with great ideas for which only they could see a market – and they will do so long into the future. Likewise, entrepreneurs will carry on starting businesses without doing any homework and corporate CEOs will lead their companies on disastrous business strategies that end up destroying shareholder value.

Each of those decisions will make perfect sense to them at the time; but if this book makes just a handful stop and ask 'Does this really add up?' then I feel it will have done some good. As Robert McMath points out in *What Were They Thinking?*:

'You are a successful product developer if you abandon ideas that are destined to fail.'

The studies I've highlighted in this book and the questions I've raised are not just for hindsight. They can be applied to every new idea, every innovation and every small business venture long before the money and the commitment get serious.

If you test your great idea against them and it flunks, my advice is to go back to the drawing board or give the whole thing up and walk away. That may not sound very helpful, but there's a sad probability that it might be the best advice you'll ever ignore.

But if you ask all the tough questions and your great idea still looks like a great idea, then my advice is 'go for it!' The world needs entrepreneurs to take risks and change the way we live. What it needs most of all, however, is for them to create innovations that succeed, not innovations that fail.

Appendix

In this book we have explored the many reasons why innovation fails, and have learnt how by asking some critical questions at an early stage such failure could have been avoided. Below is a list of 50 key questions you should ask before taking any innovation forward.

1. What problem does the innovation solve?
2. Do people perceive it as a problem?

    ● how do you know?

3. If not, at what point would it become a problem for them?
4. What was the source of the idea?

    ● finding an answer to a problem
    ● finding a new use for an existing technology
    ● it came out of market research
    ● it's following a trend
    ● you just dreamed it up.

5. Does the innovation fulfil a previously unmet need?
6. What new possibilities might it open up?
7. How do you improve your chances at the following stages of the adoption decision process?

- knowledge that the innovation exists
- recognition that it solves a problem
- influencing the adopter's decision (they may be researching it)
- the decision process itself (normally buying)
- implementation
- retention and confirmation.

8. Describe a typical early adopter. What will they want from the innovation?
9. Describe a typical late majority adopter. What will they want from the innovation?
10. How must the innovation change to move from the early adopters to the late majority?
11. Who or what will influence each group of adopters?
12. What is the old way of doing things?
13. What will adopters perceive as the relative advantage of the innovation?
14. Is it compatible with their values, experiences, culture?
15. Will users find it easy to understand?
16. Can people easily try out the innovation before committing themselves?
17. Can they observe its performance before they use it?
18. Are there risks associated with using the innovation, or does it reduce some kind of risk?
19. Does it deny people the ability to make important choices of their own?
20. Does the innovation harm or enhance the user's image?
21. Can it do the job sufficiently? If so, how?
22. How different is the innovation from things with which people might have had a good or bad experience?
23. What are the costs of adopting or switching, both in time and money?
24. What is the cost benefit to the user?
25. Does the innovation tap into any network effects?
26. Is it interoperable with rival or complementary products?
27. Is it dependent on any other innovations in order to work effectively?
28. Does the innovation create or challenge a standard?
29. Can it be built and maintained easily and cheaply?

30. Is disposal easy and cheap?
31. What inducements or subsidies exist to promote the innovation?
32. Which of these characteristics (points 14–31) will be most important to early adopters?
33. Which will be most important to the late majority?
34. Which characteristics are you, the innovator, actively promoting?
35. Is there a difference? If so, should you be worried?
36. What is the innovation's underlying Behavioural Premise?
37. What environmental clues are there?
38. In what way is the innovation different from what you see in those environmental clues?
39. What social or economic forces will drive people to adopt the innovation?
40. How will you overcome the following nebulous resistance factors:

   - 'I can't be bothered'
   - 'It's too fiddly'
   - 'I'm OK as I am'.

41. Has the innovation been the subject of excessive hype?
42. What do market forecasters predict?
43. Do you believe them? If so, why?
44. Ask someone to tell you if you show any signs of the following:

   - projecting your own needs on to users
   - excessive overconfidence
   - symptoms of groupthink
   - refusal to accept feedback or ignoring negative results from research.

45. By what criteria will you judge success?

   - market share
   - technical excellence

- customer satisfaction
- return on investment
- competitive advantage.

46. In what time frame and in what context?
47. Do you have a structured process with clearly defined criteria for Stop/Go decisions?
48. How will you sell the innovation? By promoting features or asking questions?
49. What would you do if market research showed no demand for your innovation?
50. At what point would you give up?

Further reading/Bibliography

Bobrow, Edwin E. *The Complete Idiot's Guide to New Product Development*. Alpha Books, 1997.

Bobrow, Edwin E and Shafer, DW. *Pioneering New Products*. Irwin Professional Publishing 1987.

Braun, Hans-Joachim (Guest editor). 1992. *Social Studies of Science*, (Vol 22, No. 2, Symposium on failed innovations). Sage Publications.

Brown, John Seely and Duguid, Paul. *The Social Life of Information*. Harvard Business School Press, 2000.

Cooper, Robert G. *Winning at New Products*. Perseus Publishing, 2001.

Feather, Frank. *FutureConsumer.com*. Capstone Publishing, 2001.

Gladwell, Malcolm. *The Tipping Point*. Little, Brown & Company, 2000.

Kirsch, David A. *The Electric Vehicle and the Burden of History*. Rutgers University Press, 2000.

Linacre, Vivian. *A Guide to Customary Weights and Measures*. British Weights and Measures Association, 2001.

Mackay, Charles. *Extraordinary Popular Delusions and the Madness of Crowds*, 1841. Wordsworth Editions (1995 edition).

Margolis, Jonathan. *A Brief History of Tomorrow*. Bloomsbury Publishing, 2000.

McMath, Robert M *et al. What Were They Thinking?* Times Books, 1998.

Negroponte, Nicholas. *Being Digital*. Hodder & Stoughton, 1995.

Norman, Donald A. *Things That Make Us Smart*. Perseus Publishing, 1993.

Norman, Donald A. *The Design of Everyday Things*. The MIT Press, 1998.

Norman, Donald A. *The Invisible Computer*. The MIT Press, 1998.

Rogers, Everett M. *Diffusion of Innovations*. The Free Press, 1995.

Schnaars, Steven P. *Megamistakes: Forecasting and the myth of rapid technological change*. The Free Press, 1989.

Sellen, Abigail J and Harper, Richard HR. *The Myth of the Paperless Office*. The MIT Press, 2001.

Shiller, Robert J. *Irrational Exuberance*. Princeton University Press, 2000.

Underhill, Paco. *Why We Buy: The science of shopping*. Texere, 2001.

Index